# Bernard Tickner

# A Scratch in the Soil

## edited by John Weeks

### with a Foreword by Sir Kenneth Carlisle

ISBN 978-1-5262-0694-7


published by TENTERGROUND PUBLISHING
tentergroundpublishing@gmail.com


First published May 2017

Design & Typesetting by ART$_{SLOG}$ISTIC
Printed by About Thetford Ltd

# Foreword

Bernard Tickner describes his varied life with insight, zest and humour. His is a long journey during a time of dramatic change, and readers will be grateful for this engaging memoir. The book is laced with good stories and with warmth for the people he met along the way. It is also a record of determined effort and of significant success.

Bernard has always been rooted in Suffolk. Born in 1924 and brought up in Hadleigh, he gives us the smell of that pre-war world that has gone for ever. From his earliest days he was full of pranks and mischief, traits that remained always with him. His mother's side, the Olivers, were brewers and Bernard saw his destiny in that world; but not before a typically eccentric time in the army in Africa at the end of the war.

On his return he progressed rapidly at Greene King and was the man behind their Abbot Ale. Just before he became head brewer in 1958, he found his home at Fullers Mill which was to become central to his life. As he writes, he saw 'the garden as my work and brewing as a paid holiday'. With his Norwegian wife Bess, he turned Fullers Mill into a great garden and a remarkable collection of plants, many found by them on holiday in Europe. This home was also the backdrop to a passion that embraced his life, a love of wildlife. His dogged obstinacy ensured that the gravel pits at Lackford became a nature reserve for the benefit of generations to come.

For all his success and his generosity to others, Bernard is modest about his achievements, but the outcomes speak for themselves. He was never shy of taking up the cudgels, and his intelligence and common sense saw that right prevailed. This is a compelling story of a good 'son of Suffolk'.

Kenneth Carlisle

# Editor's Preface

At first sight *A Scratch in the Soil* is a characteristically wry choice of title, for Bernard Tickner's manuscript has at its heart the sixty-year making of Fullers Mill Garden just outside West Stow village in Suffolk. Created from scratch from a poplar wood and unpromising soil beside the River Lark, the garden is now enjoyed by several thousand visitors a year as 'an extraordinary treasure-trove', 'a paradise set in seven acres'.

Seen through a wider-angle lense *A Scratch in the Soil* is equally apt as a disarming glance at ambition, the need to make and leave our mark on the world which many feel but few can satisfy. In Bernard's case, he can look back on a creative legacy in triplicate: as a brewer, he created draught Abbot Ale for Greene King; as a gardener, he and his wife Bess made Fullers Mill Garden; as a conservationist he originated Suffolk Wildlife's Lackford Lakes Reserve. Multiple marks in the sand.

And there is a third sense in which *A Scratch in the Soil* is a helpful descriptor. This book began with Bernard's desire in his mid-eighties to fix memories, to record answers to questions about the garden which he was increasingly often being asked. One thing led to another and he began to make notes on a range of subjects – people, incidents, experiences that he felt would be of interest to a wider audience. This *aide-memoire* – Bernard called it his ramblings – was dictated to Jenny Horne, Bernard's 'eyes and ears' in two tranches, the first from February 2012, the second through the winter of 2014. The latter saw some items added and others revisited and rephrased. The whole manuscript of collected paragraphs was edited and revised over the winter of 2016 when a measure of chronological and thematic structure was introduced.

So what the book is not, is an exhaustively comprehensive autobiography of a life. There are obvious omissions: little on family, school and childhood which does not relate to the development of the young naturalist. There is nothing of the introspective self-analysis and exploration of relationships that are the staple of many such works. Nor, with very few exceptions, does Bernard include living individuals among his *dramatis personae*. We have good stories, interesting facts, clear opinions and (largely) judicious comments drawn from an active life, but the essential privacy of that life is maintained. Not so much an archaeological dig; more *A Scratch in the Soil*.

John Weeks

# List of Illustrations

# Contents

# Acknowledgements

Above all I should like to thank Jenny Horne for her time and care typing the original manuscript and John Weeks for his conscientious editing.

John Foster, Nancy Curtis, Susan Chisholm, Cathy Truin, Annie Dellbridge and Heather Medcraft, David Osborne, Jan Byrne and the Hadleigh Archive, Will Cranstoun and Suffolk Wildlife Trust have provided invaluable advice, information and illustrative material in the course of the editing process. Without them the book would have been the poorer.

Its shortcomings remain my own.        B.O.T

# Picture Credits

# Chapter One

# Growing Up in Hadleigh

I was born in 1924 in Hadleigh at the Bank House in the High Street and the earliest memories I have are all connected with that house and its garden: so many sunny days amongst the flowers and trees, an enormous pear tree which had the hardest bullet-like pears you could imagine and the purple-leaved Copper Beech at the end of the garden.

I remember the enjoyment of sawing wood. I was drawn by talk of a 'saw pit' and I dug one near the rubbish dump so that the long saw could go down to its full length in the pit. There was talk, too, of a Channel Tunnel which also fascinated me and with my older brother Colin I dug under the wall near the guinea pig enclosure so that we had an easy access to the garden next door. I can't imagine how we managed to do it nor how we failed to kill ourselves in the attempt. Next door's was really a garden which had gone wild with no recognisable features of the garden left but this did not deter us. I remember sitting on the far side of the wall in this wild garden in a kind of pit with my cousin Mary, in a time that was always sunny and nice and warm and that went on and on. I must have been five or six. Altogether it was a wonderful childhood in which I was free to roam wherever I chose around the lanes and the farms without let or hindrance and later I could bicycle all the way to the villages, Elmsett, Layham and Kersey. It was magic, although I didn't realise it at the time.

The garden of Bank House was a one acre garden at the back of the Bank. It stretched beyond where it is today where the road is cut through but I remember climbing the wall at the bottom of the garden, sitting on it watching the men playing bowls on the White Lion bowling green, which they did during the summer, and watching with great interest the preparation in the spring when they treated it I think with mercury, and all the worms came wiggling up to the top. There was quite a large vegetable garden and a lawn where my brother and I used to play. Once we were playing with darts and he threw one and it got stuck in my leg and I was very alarmed. I was taken to the doctor who put my leg in the bath before he pulled the dart out and there was one very tiny little spot of blood. I was very disappointed.

We had a gardener whose name was Eli and he did a little work, not very often, and stood about a lot watering the celery. I remember him saying 'that there celery, that a water weed, that need a lot of water'. He was right, of course. It's funny how I remember that. And another memory I have is of the long line of working men queuing up for the dole – this was the late 20s, early 30s in the recession – something we could see from our drawing room windows. It filled me with sadness and my mother used to take me to help with cheap meals for the unemployed in a large hut. Oh I wish I could remember the street name but I know where it was, where they got a wholesome meal for a few coppers.

More fun was the market opposite the bank which used to take place, I think, on Mondays and was a great source of entertainment with a tremendous bustle of people, of chickens, rabbits, sheep and cattle being auctioned. It was where we sold our guinea pigs but I don't know happened to them. I hope they weren't eaten.

In the house we had a maid, Olive Beer from Layham, and a cleaning lady called Mrs Pettingale, 'Petty', who used to come in daily and then the three of us would have high tea in the kitchen and my great delight was to have something like shrimps which we peeled. A man used to come round shouting 'shrimps, Harwich shrimps'. They were small and delicious. We also had winkles with winkle pins, a small boy's delight. Milk used to be delivered every day by a horse and cart with a big milk churn and pint and quart measures on its side so we took a jug out and it would be filled with milk and brought in. In those days we had no refrigeration so as well as the milk the bread from Bloomfield's Bakery was delivered daily. There were, however, two flour mills in Hadleigh, one at Topplesfield and the other near the iron bridge. Both were of fascination to children but my brother and I weren't allowed inside them. My mother very often used to buy flour from one of the mills to make her own bread and I remember helping to knead it. I expect I made a mess of it, but I can remember now the smell of the yeast working the rising bread in the airing cupboard before it went into the oven.

At weekends, on Sundays to be precise, the Bank was shut. There were five or six Bank clerks, one being Mr Hambling, the father of the now famous Maggie Hambling, the artist, whom I remember as a little girl. My father had his Manager's Office overlooking the beds in the garden and in the evenings or on Sundays we used to unlock the big walk-in bank safe to get measured on the side of the safe wall. Whether our heights and measurement are on it still, it would be interesting to look. That's where we grew up.

Recalling Hadleigh High Street I remember Kersey's the

saddle maker and then, next to the White Lion, going up the street Richardson and Preece, suppliers of food for animals. There were all kinds of materials there. Then Eastoes the grocers and beyond that was the wonderful Partridge's, opposite Church Street, and of course Bloomfield's the bakers.

On the top floor of Partridge the ironmongers, where they sell nails and such like today, the two Miss Partridges ran a small kindergarten and my brother and I learnt to read and write there. I used to be stood in the corner regularly for not colouring things in properly. It was only years later that I discovered I was colour-blind; we never knew in those days.

In Church Street itself was the Post Office and the telephone exchange. Our number was 'Hadleigh 18' and I remember the traditional way the telephonist at the exchange would tell you 'It's no good ringing that number: they have just gone out.' She would know everything that was going on.

More or less opposite was our doctor's surgery and it was fairly rough and ready. Dr Muriel used to allow the patients to congregate outside on the pavement where they discussed their ailments quite openly amongst themselves. They would enquire from someone emerging what medicine they had been given and then would go in and ask for some of the 'pink stuff' or the 'green stuff' or suchlike – which they had great faith in.

Another place I remember in the High Street was Buckright's the hairdresser. There were two brothers and you sat on a bench waiting your turn for a six penny haircut.

I used be fascinated by the blacksmith right at the end of the High Street, where Calais Street, or Callis Street as it was always called, turned right and left to the cemetery and the hill. The ring of the anvil carried right through the High Street and was always a draw for small boys so there was quite an audience watching fascinated as the farrier ground the hot shoe on to the horse's hoof. He peeled off quite a lot of the hoof to make the shoe fit and dogs would come and eagerly seize these bits and take them off to eat.

My mother was a great organiser of children's parties and sometimes she arranged them for masses of children at the top of the barn in the White Lion's yard where there was a large room, but I enjoyed the Old Guildhall adjoining the Town Hall more. Here there was room to rampage along the boarded floor where it echoed with the noise of squealing children which was tremendous fun. I don't know if it is used today. I hope it is. I remember too the old cinema in the High Street where my father put on many different Gilbert and Sullivan operas

The Hadleigh streets were lit by gas lighting and the man used to go round on a bicycle with a pole with a hook on the end to tug open the gas lights when it was time for lighting up. We had to know what the lighting up time was, of course. It was put in the newspapers because by then you had to have a light on your bicycle or the policeman would stop you. It was some years before we had batteries for our bicycle lights but I don't remember how we lit up before then. In the High Street gutters, on both sides, was flowing water and where it came from I don't know. It was clean water but it was always flowing and there were no covers or anything so you had to be careful not to get your feet wet.

Every Sunday the Salvation Army marched from the Citadel playing like billy-o. When my father became ill my mother asked if they would stop playing as they came by the house and they readily agreed and we would just hear them softly marching by with the 'boom' 'boom' 'boom' of the drum to keep them in step. Years later, and I am talking of twenty or more years on, I happened to be in Hadleigh on Sunday afternoon and saw the Salvation Army band and sure enough it was still going by the house going 'boom' 'boom' 'boom'. I am sure they didn't know why.

# Chapter Two

# Some Family History

My mother came from the Oliver family of Sudbury where her father, my grandfather, ran with his brother the local brewery Oliver Brothers. This was situated on Cornard Road near the original Sudbury railway station and at the end of the Great War was taken over by Greene King at the suggestion of the family. Grandfather Edward, generally known as Ned, was married to Emily who died fairly young when I was a small boy and I remember vividly when my mother received the news. She was crying her heart out, and I had never seen that before. There were four children besides my mother. One sister named Vi looked after her unmarried brother Basil, who was an architect and lived in London, Arnold was a farmer and Brian, Colonel Oliver, went into Olivers Brewery before joining Greene King as Head Brewer and Director and becoming joint Managing Director in 1946. Further back, though, there was an enormous family tree with families of ten or more children, and even just including those who lived beyond infancy, Mother was one of 73 grandchildren. This seems extraordinary today, but when you consider the large families they had across a family tree in one generation and multiply up by an average of seven or eight children, it doesn't take long to get to 70 plus.

## My Grandfather

But it is about my Grandfather that I would like to write. Edward Oliver who was born in 1847, the seventh child of nine, would be known today as a character. He was known to me as a kindly old gentleman with strict ideas of how long to put up with small boys. He was fairly short, stocky and very strong and led a vigorous way of life, taking a great interest in education and the community. He was Mayor of Sudbury on several occasions and once offered the borough a piece of land for a school but it was turned down and he let it instead to a tenant farmer.

As a family we often visited Grandfather Oliver and what I enjoyed very much was the very large garden he had that was looked after by Cant who I suppose had a first name but nobody knew it. He was always known as 'Cant' except by my grandfather who called him 'Carnt'! I used to go and see Cant regularly and enjoy talking to him in the garden where there were melons and grapes as well as the usual vegetables. There was also a garden boy who did the firewood, the shoes, and other domestic errands as well but Grandfather took great delight in himself doing strenuous work with timber. He used to get a delivery of what was called cordwood in oak delivered by wagon and horses and put in the well-ventilated woodshed to dry. From time to time he would take some timber out of the shed and with a set of wedges split it on its long side before putting it back for further drying. These slices were now easier to handle when they were sawn up later as logs for the fires.

Grandfather began his day riding his horse to the Brewery early in the morning and then back for breakfast, which generally consisted of a good pint of claret and a steak. He never drank tea or coffee in his life, it was either wine or beer, though in his latter years he used to have a glass of sherry at teatime. I suppose the strenuous exercise which he enjoyed burnt off the alcohol and the food.

He was always interested in education and he paid for my brother to go on an exploration of Newfoundland with what was then called the Public School Exploration Society which included half public school boys with the rest from state schools. The Society had two main objectives: one was to introduce the two opposites of the social scale and the other was to introduce the wilderness and its wildlife to them all. Had it not been for the war I would also have taken part but as I was three years younger than my brother I missed out. (A seed may have been sown, however. In later years I had the opportunity as Rotary Foundation Chairman myself to help many young people from Bury St Edmunds to travel. Given scholarships and linked with mentors abroad, they were enabled to enrich their studies and experience in the spirit of international exploration.)

On our visits, Grandfather always wanted to know what we two boys had been doing and before leaving we were taken to see him in his study to report. He was always most receptive and when on leaving we shook hands there was always half a crown in his. As time went by this became a crown, and I've always been sorry I didn't keep one of them as a memento. There was also the promise of money when we were able to 'swim two breakwaters'. By this Grandfather meant at Felixstowe where we were at prep school. We were taken in the summer every day to swim from the beach quite near to the pier and so the prize we were aiming for came from swimming from one breakwater to the other and back again.We also used to swim at Sudbury and Hadleigh when the swimming pools were sections of the river which was in those days very clean but, of course, it was never very warm.

Grandfather also gave us an island in the river where he grew cricket bat willows – you had to take a rowing boat from the Cornard water mill up stream to get to the island – but we decided after his death that we would sell it as it was of no particular interest to us. However, Chalkpit Piece, the land which he had offered the borough for a school did prove of great interest.

Edward had made a second marriage to another Emily, whom we called Emily the Second. She was a formidable lady who had been Headmistress of a High School in Aberdeen. Although history does not relate how they met, it was probably at some kind of educational event. Emily the Second was quite commercially minded and after Grandfather's death hit upon a plan that would be tax efficient and offered Chalkpit Piece to the four grandchildren for sale. We were slightly surprised about this but she had the foresight to realise that the land would become of importance to Sudbury: as the town extended and grew it would be needed for something. Emily realised that if we bought it at agricultural rate, this would establish a much lower value than had it been for housing or some other development purpose. Then when the right time came we could sell it at a much higher rate but it would only be tax liable at its original value. My brother Colin was very hungry for cash for his new business after the war and decided to take the money but the remaining three of us were in. Eventually a compulsory purchase order came to build houses on the site. We argued the case with the tax inspector that we had no idea that this was about to happen as none of us lived locally and didn't know what was going on and nor did we see the local press – and in the end we won the day. Aunt Emily's plot did have a happy ending and was the foundation of my income today. The land is now a large housing estate at Great Cornard on the outskirts of Sudbury and there are hundreds of houses there.

## Uncle Basil

Uncle Basil lived in London in Queens Club Gardens, West Kensington, looked after by his unmarried sister, Aunt Vi.

They used to ask my brother Colin and me to stay in the holidays for a week or more at a time and they took us to all kinds of events with visits to the Tower Of London, Madam Tussauds, the Tate Gallery and the like. One thing that they always did was to take us to Regents Park Zoo on a Sunday morning because Uncle Basil was a Fellow of the Zoological Society and that meant he could go in for free with his guests with no one other than Fellows present. It was a great occasion to go behind the scenes and take various small animals out with their keepers. I remember particularly the  kinkajou, which has the ability to climb up its own prehensile tail, and a red panda. I was always more interested in the animals and birds than my brother but it all came to an end when Uncle Basil had a row with the waiters in the Fellows' lunchroom. It was really silly as on the menu were mushroom omelettes but Uncle Basil wanted them to bring him a plain omelette. They just wouldn't do it, so he resigned his fellowship over a mushroom omelette! It was a great pity but we still went to the Zoo to see the gibbons, the seals, the eagles and other big birds of prey, and the birds in the tropical house, all of which I loved. I knew all the names and many more besides.

As well as to the zoo and the other sights, we went to all the theatres and there was a box of chocolates every time which was a delight for young boys. Basil made going to any event exciting by planning the most complicated route possible, travelling by bus, underground, taxi and on foot, and he enjoyed the challenge of working it all out so that we arrived at the right place at the right time. This generally worked very well but on one occasion it overcame him: he told us to jump onto a train which was on the point of departure, and it was only after we had been in it a while that we discovered it was a non-stop train to Southend when we should have been in Central London! Mostly, however, he was very accurate and a great fan of the information in Bradshaw's Guide, still going strong in the 1920s and 30s.

Uncle Basil was an architect, a Fellow of the Royal Institute of British Architects, and ran his own business from the apartments in the block of flats he lived in. The blocks were named alphabetically. His was near the end and was called Unwin Mansions and there was a garden in the centre of the square outside his apartment. He was always meticulous in his work and his beautiful plans for housing developments and private houses were hand coloured and works of art in themselves. He was a staunch supporter of the Art Workers' Guild and the Art Nouveau movement and was a great friend of Lutyens. Quite a lot of his buildings were pubs or municipal buildings and locally in Bury St Edmunds they include the original Borough of St Edmundsbury Offices on Angel Hill and the so called Pillar of Salt signpost in front of the Angel Hotel.

Basil Oliver was quite well known and in those days a Fellow only received that title when he had earned it, so he could pick and choose his clients. Once a client had agreed a scheme design and Basil had done the last bit of paperwork down to the last door handle, which he always specified, there would be no change. So if a client then said 'Do you think we could have a window looking out on the garden side?' he would say 'Yes, of course. But you will need a new architect as well'.

All this would not have been possible without the support of Aunt Vi who looked after Uncle Basil and his guests so well – including us, of course – until his death in 1948. After Basil's death she moved to a purpose-built house in Great Cornard. After a period of estrangement, she was reunited with Emily the Second and they became great pals. Aunt Vi established a very good garden and we still have plants from her that are growing at Fullers Mill today.

### The Tickner Family

As a family I knew a lot about the Olivers but the strangest thing is that neither I nor my brother knew anything about my father's family except that we had two maiden aunts who lived in Ipswich. We used to see them fairly regularly. They lived in a flat owned by a Mrs Parrott, whom we were always taken to see when we visited, but we never enquired of them about any one else in the family and I now rather regret it. The only thing that was said in a jokey kind of way was that our antecedents were sheep stealers and cattle rustlers on Romney Marsh in Kent, perhaps the eighteenth century Tickners whose family history lay behind Russell Thorndike's *Doctor Syn* stories.

Some years later, visiting Kent to look at gardens with my

friend Bettye Reynolds, I travelled along the sea road between Rye and Dungeness. This was land which during the war was full of Artillery sites with regiments that included the one I was in, and will describe later, there to shoot down doodlebugs as they came in over the sea. By the time Bettye and I travelled through, however, the old sites had been excavated for gravel all along the Romney Marsh. Now as we drove round the area we discovered in Brenzett a signpost to Tickner's Lane. At a nearby junction there was a church with a wedding service in progress. We didn't stop to look at the tombstones but I expect the churchyard was full of Tickners. This led me to wonder whether it was possible to discover who the Tickners were and Bettye looked them up on a website called Findmypast. This yielded information which none of us had before – that my father had four sisters, two of whom we knew, and one brother. We discovered that Leonard had been a medical student at Durham University and we then asked the Archive Department at the University whether they had any information. They confirmed what we already knew but could add nothing fresh, so what happened to Leonard is a mystery. He was never mentioned by my father.

Uncle Leonard has disappeared without trace, but I am glad to know of this history – which does not carry any of the sinister attachments which at one time we imagined when no one ever talked about it other than the two maiden aunts. So thank goodness for a fairly respectable family history.

# Chapter Three

# The Young Naturalist

I have often wondered why I became interested in wildlife. It didn't come from the garden for while I enjoyed that as a place in which to be, I did not enjoy any work I was given to do there. I hated holding the basket when father picked the brussels sprouts for Christmas dinner on a cold winter morning or standing for ages picking strawberries or raspberries. Nor was I impressed by pets. I think we had a tortoise who managed to live for many years hibernating in the garden. We did keep guinea pigs at home and the family had to look after them whilst we were away at school but they never held much interest for me: they either needed feeding or clearing out or both and they don't do much in return. No, it began with the love of wild plants which grew on walks in the countryside, country lanes and woods. My mother certainly encouraged this interest and every year took me on bicycle rides to get bunches of primroses in a wood near Hadleigh; we always tied them up with wool. We also went bluebelling, but this was never as good because the stems oozed a vicious type of juice and they wilted. The thrill of a primrose wood, however, has never left me.

I got to know my wildflowers, or at least the English names of them, from a very early age and then when I stayed with my friend Hugh Pulham, my horizons were broadened. Hugh's family rented the Valley Farm, Framsden from the Tollemache estate and in the low meadows were thousands of fritillaries. It was a common plant in the valley bottoms in those days and I expect it was fritillaries all the way all through that valley to Boundary Farm where the Suffolk Wildlife Trust now has its Fritillary Meadow. I dare say if the land was treated in the traditional way again they would re-emerge. It would be marvellous if those days could be recreated for small boys to be able to pick wild flowers when they were so abundant but I fear it is now too late to recapture that golden dream.

The Pulhams' farmhouse was a delight. Mrs Pulham did a weekly bake with a faggot heating the oven in the back kitchen and in would go all the pies – apple pie, steak and kidney pie, you name it. The pies were was followed by the bread for the week. The homemade bread was delicious as was the farmhouse butter Mrs Pulham made in the dairy. Rather salty and slightly rancid with water droplets oozing from it, it had a flavour I have never encountered since. There was no electricity in the house and it was candles to go to bed with. They must have been the kind of conditions that the Victorians and the earlier generations had for hundreds of years.

As I grew older I spent a lot of time on the farms in Hadleigh. My favourite was the one near Wolves Wood on the outskirts of Hintlesham. We used to bicycle there and I liked it because it was a glorious muddle. The farmer, I think it was Mr Turner, wasn't very good at farming, I suspect, but I didn't realise that in those days. All I know is that I was always made welcome and I could go and see the horses in the stable. Later on I used to ride the horses, good old Suffolk Punches, on their way to the harvest field. The corn was cut and put into shocks and when it was dry and loaded on the wagon I used to ride the horse back to the stack yard where the stack was being made. I expect it would have got there on its own but I used to like to think I was in charge of it. Then the horses as they came in from work were led to the horse pond which they just walked into and drank from before they went to the stables to be fed.

When I was old enough, I suppose twelve or thirteen, I used to work on Mr Mudd's farm at Shelley in the holidays. Mostly it was mucking out the cattle yard where deep litter had been accumulating all winter. It would be taken out in tumbrils, and hard work it was loading it and putting it into a stack before it was spread on the fields. The other job we did was singling sugarbeet with a hoe. I would have my own line alongside the long rows of working men. This was before 'monogerm' had been invented and the beet had to be singled to allow room for growth. Later on it had to be chopped out so that one good beet would appear in the space available for it. After that you had to clean the land with the hoes. These were sharpened with a file which made it much easier. You would catch your lunchtime break in the hedge, normally it was cold tea and sandwiches, and you could hear the church clock ringing out the hours from the fields. I loved it. It was great fun and the men were very nice to me.

When I was older again, about fifteen or sixteen, I used to work on a fruit farm in the summer. I think it was called Town End. Here grew all the old apple varieties, at a time when Cox's Orange was really a wonderful tasting apple, unlike the modern version which is more regular but has lost its character. They also grew Ellison's Orange Pippin, a spicy and delicious fruit. I find it interesting that the way in which apples are picked hasn't changed since those days, sixty or more years ago. They are still picked into a 'hod', a container with a fabric base which is strapped to your chest. When you have filled it, the apples can be let down gently into a big box to be collected by the tractor. It is an easy way to avoid bruising.

All in all, I suppose with all these early experiences it was only natural that I took to the country life when I was able to pursue my own way of doing things. But watching a television programme recently in which David Attenborough talked about his early days set off a whole train of memories from my youth and suggested another stream of influences on me.

It was whilst my parents went on holiday that I was sent to my great friends the Voyces, at their big house and garden at Benton Way, on the same side as Benton End, the house of the painter and iris breeder Cedric Morris, but nearer Hadleigh itself. In my youth Benton End itself was strictly out of bounds. 'Artists lived there', it was said, and that explained everything. It was only later on when I was adult that I got to know Cedric who was a generous and fine gardener. Many plants today owe their existence to his influence and introductions. It is good to know that many of his irises have been collected by Sarah Cook and are available for sale today.

The Voyces had, I thought, a magic garden with a willow wood and a sandy hill with lavender and citrus bushes growing, as well as a low barn, pastures with cattle, a switchback railway and a swimming pool. There were two sons and the one I liked was John who was my hero and took me everywhere with him. I suppose I was about six or seven years old, he several years older. We had both fallen under the spell of the pioneer wildlife photographer and author Cherry Kearton and I remember the books about animals that we were both reading in 1934 (in which same year David Attenborough was being inspired watching one of Kearton's wildlife films). John and I for our part were inspired to set out to tame an already docile cow in the meadow. The idea was to be able to ride her. As far as I can remember, this never came about because any attempt to sit on her was resisted; I think in the end we gave up.

Another thing I remember from staying at the Voyces was reading a book called *The Enchanted Garden* by Henry James Forman. I remember going to sleep every night with this book. I hadn't finished it by the time I left to go home so I pestered my mother to buy it for me so that I could finish it. I believe this book, too, played a part in developing my lifelong interest in wildlife.

Not all my memories of the Voyces involve wildlife or, indeed, are as happy. I remember, for instance, being afraid of John's father, Colonel Voyce, mainly because he taught me to swim and his method was tying a strap underneath my armpits and suspending this from a rope on a pole. On the introduction of my body to the water, the pole could be lifted to keep me afloat whilst I went through the motions of swimming. Then, when he thought I was doing well, he would dip the tip of the pole, whereupon I sank spluttering and had to be lifted back up again. This was a cruel way from which a 'swimmer' had no escape: it was very much a case of sink or swim. I hated it and the Colonel as well. The thing that did make me swim in the end was the promise of my grandfather's five shilling reward for 'two breakwaters'!

And one embarrassing memory. Every afternoon tea was served in a large conservatory and one day there were several family friends there as well. Whilst I was sitting on the floor on the skin of a lion – it had a large head, I remember – I must have decided one of the guests was extremely beautiful and I was staring at her with admiration. Then to my dismay I discovered that everyone in the room was looking at me with smiles on their faces, watching my reaction to the beautiful lady. I was caught. I blushed to the roots of my hair with embarrassment – and I believe that was the last time I ever blushed, because I don't know how to do it anymore.

Despite the awkward moments, however, I am grateful that it was at the Voyces that I discovered Cherry Kearton, whose work probably triggered something in me, as in David Attenborough, which made me interested in the natural world. From then on I grabbed every chance of reading about animals and birds and butterflies and moths. I fear I have to say that, like so many small boys of that era, I also used to go bird-nesting in the hedgerows to get sparrow and chaffinch eggs, but we only took the one and I think I gave it up after a time when I switched to butterflies and moths which then became my obsession. I had a cabinet and I collected them avidly and in fact bred several kinds. There was a disused aviary where I had a whole colony of buff tips and I loved the Puss Moth caterpillar and then all the hawk moth family – Eyed Hawk, Poplar Hawk and the rest. The hobby lasted until I went into the army at 18 years old; I never collected any more and I gave all my collection away to a young friend who I knew was interested. I am not proud of it but it seemed part of the learning one went through living in the country, though it may now be seen as indefensible in today's ecological climate.

It will not be surprising that when people asked what I was going to be when I grew up I used to reply 'I am going to be a vet'. I imagine somebody, recognising my love for animals, said 'you ought to be a vet' and in my innocence I supposed the two things compatible. But I now know better. A vet has to be pragmatic about making his decisions for the benefit of the animal he is treating and for the benefit of his client, whom he ought to know well. Some vets get the balance wrong and treat the client rather than the animal.

# Chapter Four

# The Young Brewer

In 1940 I left Framlingham School when it moved inland to Repton in Derbyshire, where it would be safer in case of a German invasion, the threat of which was at that time very real. My Uncle Brian, who was a director and Head Brewer at Greene King in Bury St Edmunds, said that if I wanted to do so I could join the company to learn some basic brewing. It was necessary to get two years' practical experience prior to taking the three year course at the Birmingham Brewing School. Starting now would enable me to get this training in before I had to join up and if I came back after the war I would then be in a position to go to the brewing school. So this is what I did. I had three wonderful years, beginning at the age of 16 by running the recently completed Brewhouse in Bury St Edmunds with Margaret, Uncle Brian's daughter, and brewing extremely weak beer because of the shortage of every material you could think of, including the coal needed to raise steam.

Then at the age of 17 I was sent to run the brewery in Cambridge, in Panton Street, whilst the Head Brewer was on holiday. He was an ex-Oliver's man from Sudbury and seemed to me extremely ancient. I remember he had a dew drop on the end of his nose and drank his tea from a teaspoon, as it was very hot. He said he did this because he had piles, but exactly what the connection was between the two I never discovered. I watched him avidly in the hope that before he could get the next spoonful in a dewdrop would in fact drop, but at the last second he always sniffed and it was all over.

I was in digs in Silver Street. Today the building is part of Darwin College, the graduate college established in 1964, but in my day it housed a mixture of elderly members of the University and youngsters like me, all at separate tables, guarding their ration of jam, sugar and butter without speaking to each other; it was dreadful. I had to bicycle from there every day along the Fen Causeway in the early morning with the wind blowing from Siberia to 'mash in'. At the time I thought I was running the Brewery but the truth, I suspect, is that it would have run perfectly well without my intervention and everyone politely declined to say so.

Among the stories of the Panton Street Brewery I picked up was that of a predecessor of mine at the Brewery, a keen fisherman, who had caught some trout and put them alive in the water tank over the front porch. Alas, at the weekend one of the trout got sucked into the exit which became blocked, the tank overflowed and water poured down to the room underneath. Unfortunately, this happened to be the tobacco stores and the entire supply of cigarettes earmarked for the pubs was ruined. He was not a very popular man after that. Another tale concerned the habit in the Brewhouse of discharging the copper into the hop-back just before lunch so that it settled during the lunch period; then, when everyone came back from lunch, it was ready to pump up to be refrigerated into the fermenting vessels. However, one day when they came back they found there was nothing in the hop-back because someone had forgotten to shut the valve. They quickly reassembled everything and did another mash in record time before the excise officer knew what had happened: they got away with it. Another trick they had depended on the fact that one of the fermenting vessels had a loose copper lining. After the dip had been taken and registered in the Excise book there would be a great regurgitatation and with a sound I can only describe as 'gerlumph' echoing around the Brewery, the lining would be forced back. More liquid would enter the vessel and a few hundred pounds of duty would be saved.

Not such a happy ending to the other story I was told, that one of the former owners of the Brewery used to enjoy revolver practice on the Brewing Room door, so that it paid to knock very loudly before entering. Eventually he used to go around the Brewery and if he saw something he didn't like he shot at it. If the temperature was wrong, he shot at the thermometer and so on. Tragically, at the end he shot all his family and himself.

I was also sent for some time to Furneux Pelham, near Bishop's Stortford, where there was an even smaller Brewery called Rayment & Co which belonged to Greene King. Whereas Cambridge was run by a vice-admiral, Vice-Admiral Lake, Pelham was run by an ex-Captain RN Submarines, Neville Lake, who was an enormous character. He was a Roman Catholic who built a little church at his house and recruited the coxswain of his submarine to be his sales manager and converted him to Roman Catholicism as well. He then set him on selling Guinness to all the Roman Catholic Clubs between Pelham and the Thames, which was hugely successful. Neville Lake was always suspicious of me in later years, thinking I was the one who was going to close Pelham. He couldn't understand why I thought running the milk from the dairy through the brewery pasteuriser was a bad idea, either. I have memories, too, of the Captain standing on the deck of the combine harvester as it went round the fields bringing in the harvest from the Pelham Brewery farm; he hoped to sell us the yield to be malted but, embarrassingly, we always had to turn it down because of poor quality.

One day when I was in Neville's office I asked him what the map with little flags showed, expecting that it would be where we had accounts, but in reality it was the progress of asphalting gangs paid for by the County Council to resurface roads. He took a great interest in this because when a gang was near a pub car park he asked the cashier to give him a handful of five pound notes and out he would go to dish them out to the men and ask them to include the car park as they went past. Captain Lake was much loved by all concerned in the brewery although his method of management was mistrusted at HQ by his brother Lancelot, Major Lake, the Managing Director.

There is just one more Pelham story which needs telling. There had been a robbery in the Wine and Spirits store by a London gang who had taken quite a lot of the stock so it was decided to hire a night watchman. The only person that they could think of was a man called Herbie Warner, who lived in a hedge on the outskirts of Pelham in part of an old aircraft which he had purloined from somewhere. So they brought Herbie in and decided to lock him in the office at night because they didn't trust him walking about. He was given a training course by the Head Brewer who said

'I am going down to the Brewery telephone exchange and then I want you to lift the receiver, introduce yourself and pretend to tell me what you see outside in the yard.'

Herbie made his call.

'I'm Herbie Warner and I've lived here all my life...'

Having then been given the correct form of words, Herbie tried again and Bill Hynard the Head Brewer replied, in character,

'The police station here.'

'My God!' said Herbie, putting the phone down. 'The police are here! I'm off!'

He was brought back, however, and the training went on.

The night watchman scheme was partially successful but in the end they put in a burglar alarm system and also got the police to monitor the premises at different times during the night. Inevitably, one dark night the alarm went off and people emerged from houses all around, Bill in his gum boots with a 12 bore gun and others armed with cudgels and a variety of weapons, all converging on the wine store. At this moment a police car arrived to survey the site and as its headlamps swept across the scene they picked out a large number of armed people whom the police took to be burglars. The car swept out again rapidly, the officers calling for reinforcements. The truth of the matter was that a rat had eaten through the alarm cable and caused all the trouble.

## Management Style

Meanwhile at Bury I was learning not only how to brew beer but to understand Management and at that time the

33

company was run on strict military lines. All the directors had military titles from Captain through to Colonel: 1940 was not so long after the Great War had finished but none of these gentleman were young enough to serve in the current war at that time. In the lower ranks of the brewery were foremen who were all ex-sergeants and sergeant majors with charge hands who were former corporals and bombardiers. Every Friday afternoon there was a meeting at which the foremen, arranged in a row, reported to the Head Brewer and Managing Director on what was happening, who was sick and the like. They were then dismissed one by one and the junior managers were interviewed, me at the bottom of all this pecking order. This was followed on Saturday mornings with a parade round the brewery led by Major Lake, the Managing Director, sometimes in hunting pink. He was followed by the Head Brewer, second brewer, third brewer and me, with messages sent down the line to do something about whatever it was had caught his eye.

The militaristic approach, I hardly need to say, was not enjoyed by those on the receiving end of it. I remember, for example, another young brewer whose name was Stebbings who was learning to brew before returning to his small company, I think in Lowestoft. He and I both had to wear a white coat and cloth cap when at work. In London this was a bowler hat in winter and a straw boater in summer but the fashion in the countryside was different. You were, however, expected to wear the uniform all the time. One day we were both outside in the street and Stebbings had not got his cap on when the Major appeared, advancing down the pavement. I said to Stebbings 'You are for it, my lad' and sure enough the Major raised a finger and beckoned to him and he crossed over to meet him. The conversation went like this:

'Morning, Stebbings.'

'Morning, sir.'

'You are not wearing your cap.'

'No, sir.'

'Why aren't you wearing it?'

'Don't know, sir.'

After considering this, the Major came out with the wonderful reply: 'Well, how do y' think you'll be able to raise it to me, if you are not wearing it?'

It further illustrates the situation during the early part of the war and the Major's loyal response of grim determination and sense of the immediacy of the fighting that he used to order all the young people to come to the Brewhouse every few months where he addressed them from on high. 'My boys,' – there were no girls – 'there's a war on and we are all going to do our bit, aren't we?' And to a chorus of 'Yes, sir,' he continued 'I want you to join either the Red Cross, the ARP (Air Raid Precautions), the Home Guard, the fire watchers or a similar organisation, and tell me what that is, if you want to stay in the company.' He made sure everyone did join up to do something.

Lancelot Lake was at heart, however, a very kind and charitable man; in spite of being a great autocrat he was very sensitive to the hard luck endured by many of the employed people. And others. A typical example of this occurred immediately after the war had ended. Most companies at the time, where they could, found places for men returning from the front – many their previous employees, of course – but Lance Lake saw further. I can hear him saying to me now 'We should look after the returning officers', realising that their position made it no easier for them to find employment. Accordingly he arranged, without his influence being known to them, that two officers should be appointed as brewers in Bury and Cambridge respectively. Significantly, one officer was from the Army, one from the Navy.

For Lake, the Air Force was too young a service to be considered. Coincidentally, the man who got his start at Panton Street, John Rowley, later became Head Brewer at Young's Ram Brewery where he will figure in later pages of this book.

E.L.D. Lake was Mayor of Bury St Edmunds on nine occasions and an Honorary Freeman of the Borough. He ran the town and the Brewery as one enterprise, saying often 'What is good for the Brewery is good for the town and vice versa'. It was said that civil servants who came from Cambridge to Bury were very much afraid of the Major. They called it the 'the Lake District'.

The military formality ran through the company and certainly extended to the boardroom. I remember that when Sir Edward Greene was Chairman we used to have the AGM at a long table which would be turned round so that the Directors sat on one side of it. Then a few lines of chairs were brought in so that a dozen or so 'trusties' could be invited to be the public with the indomitable Miss Lake, the major's twin sister, sitting in the front row and others deploying themselves in descending order of rank. The meeting consisted of Sir Edward inviting Directors to reappoint themselves and they popped up and down repeating the phrase 'Ladies & gentleman, I am pleased to propose the re-election of Mr so and so,' which duly took place. One day, however, someone settling an old score instead of repeating the refrain began 'Ladies & gentleman, it is with the greatest reluctance I propose the re-election of Mr –.' It startled everybody but they still raised their hands in approval of the appointment.

At ordinary board meetings long serving employees came in at the end to receive either a gold watch or a clock as they chose. One truly memorable occasion featured the old foreman horseman, who had looked after the last remaining horses and had been the groom in Sir Edward's day, growing up with him since a boy, so the pair knew each other extremely well. By this time, aged 65, the old foreman was extremely deaf and come the day of his presentation, General Sir Miles Dempsey, who was in the process of taking over as chairman from Sir Edward, was half way through a citation when the foreman said in a very loud, deaf-sounding voice 'Where's Teddy?', meaning Sir Edward. The General, startled, replied 'I am very sorry. Sir Edward couldn't be here today,' to which the foreman replied 'Gittin too old for it, I s'pus'. Then, when it was time to hand over the clock he interrupted again with 'Do that chime?' There was a hurried consultation and to everyone's relief the answer was yes.

In time the AGM was moved to the Georgian Theatre Royal, across the road from the Brewery. Here we all sat with the drop curtain at our backs and everyone knew that on the stage, which was a very large one, were two bars of drinks and eats. This mouth watering set was deliberately calculated to shorten the length of the AGM. In Sir Edward's day he used to achieve this by saying 'This concludes the business of the meeting and as there are no further questions it is now closed,' but democracy had to win and now there was a short interval between asking whether there were any questions and the close.

Hugh Greene, when he was Chairman, used to stand out in front and seek out questions. He used to relish the cut and thrust of debate which he was used to at the BBC where he was Director General. We, on the other hand, all squirmed when somebody wanted to know about something which, in their view, hadn't been properly done. When Jonnie Bridge was Chairman, however, he managed to get the AGM done and dusted in seven minutes flat. If no one asked a first question, you could shut the meeting down but if a first question was put, it was always followed by more. So in the short interval which followed the call for questions, a good sense of timing was essential. As far as I know Jonnie holds the record. It's all gone badly wrong since then and scores of questions are asked to satisfy the egos of those putting them. In the good old days a trusty would simply be asked to thank the Chairman for running the meeting and the Board for being so clever at improving the profits and dividends once again.

The clamber up from auditorium to stage was a hazardous game and eventually holding the AGM at the Theatre Royal had to be abandoned under the sheer weight of people wanting to attend the meeting. It had become an important part of the social round in Bury and its surrounding catchment so the occasion was moved to Culford School where there was a lot more room and car parking was much easier. This allowed the numbers to grow yet more, and as they did the buffet was more severely rationed, but it all came to an end when for some reason the school wished to divide up the hall and it became of no practical use to us. The AGM then moved to the Rowley Mile on Newmarket Racecourse where it remains to this day.

### Brewery Horses

In the early 1940s Greene King still had a few dray horses left, with a foreman drayman in charge. The drays were wagons constructed so that they could take racks of casks of different sizes: barrels of 36 gallons, kilderkins of 18 gallons, firkins of 9 gallons and, unusually, pins of 4.5 gallons. These would be slung out on to the deck of the dray and stacked at 45 degrees which enabled clips to be put on the ends of a cask at the point of delivery. The cask was then lifted so that it could be positioned either directly in the cellar or on to the skids and slid gently down.

One day a dray arrived at The Castle pub in Bury, so it hadn't had very far to go, but when it got there it was discovered that one or perhaps more of the wheels had become locked and the steel tyres had been worn flat. What had happened was that between the brewery and the pub they had failed to take off the brake (the brake consisting only of a rope put round one of the back wheels and secured tightly on the dray). I asked the head drayman how they had travelled so far like that when the horse would have had to lean into an unusually heavy load and the noise of the wheels screeching must have been terrible. Surely they would they have noticed something; and the head drayman said without a smile on his face

'Why, they were drunk, weren't they.'

'At that time in the morning?'

'Yes. They had had too many.'

I don't know how they got back to the brewery on a flat tyre.

Horses are very sensitive to the routine of delivery: the order of pubs never changed and the animals knew when and where they were going on to each one until it was time to go back home. In between they delivered the load and picked up the empties, a sequence that never varied. As they delivered, the load lessened and the pull was different. The empties came on and the pull was different again. Eventually they could feel that the day's work was done: they had been to the last pub on the round, delivered the load and picked up the empties. All they needed now was the confirmation 'Go hoom, boy' and the drayman could put the reins in his lap and go to sleep while the good old horse went home. The drayman didn't wake until they were back at the brewery. The system worked extremely well with horses but come the day of conversion to lorries came a big change in the drayman's life. He had to learn how to drive and he had to stay awake the whole time. Sometimes this was forgotten and after the last delivery he would go to sleep as usual, only to find himself in the ditch shortly after. This happened on many occasions until the training took over.

The horses, however, always knew how far they had got on a journey and when they were home, and they were trained on their return to relieve themselves in a large drain in the brewery yard – it is still there between the old offices and the sample room on the south side of Westgate Street. When the horses reached that spot the drayman whistled and the result was a couple of gallons down the drain. This kept the quarters cleaner than they would have been and then the horses were free to gallop past their stables on the right down to the meadows to graze. The meadows were where the winestore was built in 1974, south of Westgate Street alongside the old bowling green, running down to the water meadows and the River Linnet. The old stables are still there, used as storage units, opposite the Brewery Tap.

## Two Tales

Our first Security Manager was a Sergeant newly retired from the Police Force. He was the best we ever had, even though on his retirement the new Security Manager was a police rank higher and on his retirement a rank higher and so on until, I forget now but I believe, the last that I knew had been a Police Inspector.

Well, the Sergeant knew everybody and was extremely vigilant from the ground up. He would have confidential talks with people, drawing them to one side so he could see what was going on with regard to his main concern of the moment. At one such moment he asked to have a talk with me which began

'Worried about the Rowley Mile, sir.'

'Are you, Sergeant? Why is that?'

'All that grass, sir.'

I just said 'Oh yes', because it was the first occasion on which the annual staff party and dinner dance was to be held

40

there and I couldn't see the connection. And then he said

'And it's dark, sir.'

'Yes, it will be. So what's the problem?'

'They will all be at it, sir.' And when I laughed he said 'Is there a company policy on 'cope-ulation?'' – as he pronounced it.

I said that I did not know but I would find out from Sir Hugh Greene and I duly asked the Chairman if we had a policy on cope-ulation. Sir Hugh laughed and thought for a bit and said of course we did. I replied that I had never heard of it, what was it, please? And he said with considerable gusto

'Let's have more of it!'

I said I couldn't possibly tell the Sergeant that, he would be mortified, and Sir Hugh came back,

'Tell him something to hold the situation.' I asked what he meant. 'Well,' said the Chairman, 'tell him we are thinking about it', adding wickedly with a glint in his eye, 'all the time'.

So that is what I told the Sergeant and it seemed to satisfy him.


The boiler men at the Brewery were all ex-Navy stokers, immensely reliable when it came to producing steam on time from their impeccably maintained machinery but less concerned with the technicalities of the operation One such stalwart, Suffolk born and bred, was on duty in the Boiler Room when a party of visitors arrived to view its array of gleaming brass boilers, pipes, valves and large dials. The group ended up in front of one such dial with a pointer that could be swung between the letters A and H. Making conversation, one of the party asked what the letter A stood for.

'Well, A – that stand for 'and controlled,' the boiler man replied.

'And H?'

'That stand for hautomatic.'

## 'Mr Coovny'

Percy Coveney was the celebrated Head Brewer of Adnams Brewery and he was celebrated for two reasons. Firstly he brewed excellent beer and won numerous prizes in competitions. Secondly he loved his product so much that he used to drink quite a lot of it.

All this came vividly to light when years ago I went to a Brewers' Guild dinner at Southwold. I sat next to one of their old and bolds who had just been promoted to Brewer status. He was an old servant of the mash tun: I expect he was the brewhouse foreman who in his old age had been elevated to the position so he put his best suit on and his best uncomfortable shoes to come to the dinner. After a bit I thought of asking him about Mr Coveney and eventually I asked him

'Is it true that Mr Coveney had a pin of beer put up for him at his home everyday? And that if that he couldn't manage the four and half gallons [36 pints] on his own, he would invite a few friends in to help him out of a muddle?'

'Well,' he said, 'Mr Coovny, he did like his drop of beer, but that weren't his main claim to fame.'

I said 'Wasn't it? What was it, then?'

'Well, Mr Coovny, he were a very nice gentleman but he a-keep fallin' in hooles.'

'Why was that?'

'Well, he only 'ad little ol' legs, see! And he were a bit top 'eavy. Once in the brewery they were a-clenin out the main drain and Mr Coovny, he come along to see and stood near the drain and looked in. "What are doin' 'ere, boys?" he asked and he must 'av just leaned over too far and he toppled right in up to his waist in water, so we had to take him hoom to dry 'im out.' Apparently another time Percy went to see the launching of the new lifeboat at Southwold and again he leant a bit too far forward to get a

42

better view, toppled right into the sea and had to be rescued. So I asked whether it was anything to do with all his drinking.

'No, no, no, no, no. That was nuthin' to do with drinkin'. The reason Mr Coovny would a-keep fallin' in hooles was nuthin' to do with his drinking. No, no, no, no,no. His main problem was he'd only got little ol' legs, see? He hadn't got noo centa a-grav'ty.'

My Southwold neighbour went on to tell me how on one occasion Mr Coveney had been out with his friends around the pubs and when it was time to go home they found it difficult to keep him upright. He tended to fall over all the while so one of them went back to the pub and asked the landlady if he could borrow a bit of carpet. They put it on the ground and rolled Mr Coveney up. They took him along horizontally and made good progress and eventually got to his home. They rang the bell and Mrs Coveney came to the door.

'Hello, boys. What have you got there, then?'

'Well, mam. We've brought Mr Coovny hoom. What shall we do with him?' and she said

'Roll him out along the hall, will you.'

And that is what they did, as though it was the most natural thing to happen in the world!

'Another time', he went on, 'it was at the funeral of one of the Mr Adnams and everyone had been to the church and then he was carried to the graveside and lowered in and one by one the gentlemen there would step forward and each give a little nod in his respect to say farewell. And that come to Mr Coovny's turn and he stepped forward to the graveside, took his booler 'at orf and gave a little nod and, would you believe it, toppled right in with a big thump. He was a-shouting and a-hollerin "Git me out of here, boys. I broke my bloody leg," an they 'ad to get the gravediggers' ladder to lift him out to take him to the hospital.'

So I gently enquired again whether it was all the drink that caused this.

'No, no, no. His main problem was he'd only got little ol' legs, see, and he hadn't got noo centa a-grav'ty'.

Percy Coveney continued to win many prizes and the many trips to Olympia for the presentations used to be celebrated with gusto. Coming back to Liverpool Street station on the bus, said my friend, it was hilarious because they would be sitting at the back with the seats facing inwards and whenever they went around a corner they would shout out 'Hold on to Mr Coovny' because his feet didn't reach the ground and he would topple out onto the gangway. When they got back to Southwold there were wonderful celebrations and I remember Michael Loftus, brother of the Chairman of Adnams and himself the founder of Woottens Nursery at Wenhaston, showing me a photograph of everyone in the Brewery in the yard with the Adnams family and the Loftus family celebrating the return of Mr Coveney and giving him three cheers. It is a wonderful photograph of a very happy time. After his retirement in latter years Percy went into a Nursing Home but I am glad to say Adnams Brewery continued to send beer for him to the Home, not a pin, but a case of bottled beer for the rest of his life.

And at the end of that evening of stories, I asked the old Brewer yet again whether he thought all that beer drinking had affected Mr Coveney's falling in holes.

'Oh no,' he said, 'that weren't the main problem. 'Is main problem was that he'd only got little ol' legs and he hadn't got noo centa a-grav'ty'!

### Graham Greene

Sir Hugh's brother the novelist Graham Greene used to come to visit the brewery quite frequently and I used to sit whilst

he told me about various things happening to him and particularly about the person whom he always called the Other who used to impersonate him around the world. The trick was that, because most people had heard of Graham Greene but hardly anyone knew what he looked like, all the Other had to do was to mug up on Greene's books and any personal details he could get hold of and put on a fine display of authority so that he would be received in a foreign capital and wined and dined. This annoyed Graham a great deal and particularly so once when he was visiting Chile. When he flew in to Santiago he was accused of impersonating himself, because the Other had just left the country after a week of wining and dining and literary lunches. It was only with the greatest difficulty that he managed to persuade the Chileans that he was the right person. Perhaps even more irritating, however, was that once a year *The Times Literary Supplement* organised a competition inviting readers to write a piece of so many words in the style of Graham Greene. Graham used to enter this regularly, but to his annoyance he never won.

One year I read a piece in one of the trade journals which described how a Brewery in San Francisco by the name of Wilde had brewed a special beer to commemorate Oscar, although it had no association with him other than the name. The brew was a great success, particularly amongst the homosexual community, so I suggested that we should brew a Graham Greene special and he was thrilled at the idea. A special label was created which he signed and he came in the early morning to start the brew himself. This beer was sold over the years in various ways, which included a presentation package with the novel *Brighton Rock*. I remember asking Graham which sector of the market his brew would be appreciated by and without hesitation he said the heterosexual section – he was rather well known for having a wife in every port.

A final Greene story: the two brothers Graham and Hugh were at University in Cambridge together and during that time they used to take a great interest in beers of every description. They used to take notes on different Breweries and the quality of their ales. During a discussion one day Graham asked me what McMullen's beer was like and I said it had greatly improved. He said he remembered the time when he and Hugh went into a McMullen's pub on a rather dreary kind of day and there was just one man in the bar standing by the window. The licencee, in a fairly desperate attempt to enliven the atmosphere, said cheerily

'It looks like rain,' and the chap at the window said

'Yes, and it tastes like piss.'

But these excursions into Greene-land have taken me some way beyond 1940, to which we must now return. Taking Lancelot Lake to heart, I was already kitted out with army uniform and crucially had boots which were worn in and polished to within an inch of their lives. I had joined the Home Guard.

# Chapter Five

# A Military Man

### The Home Guard

As all my family had been in the Royal Artillery I was allocated to one of the two Home Guard platoons in Bury St Edmunds who were called the Gunners because at the bottom of Rougham Hill and on Eastgate Street there were gun emplacements, sited where the railway crossed the road. An anti-tank ditch had been dug all along the railway line so that an unsuspecting tank coming over the railway would, it was hoped, drop into this ditch and be unable to get out. However, a tank could get through without meeting the ditch under the railway bridges where the track crossed the road on Rougham Hill and in Eastgate Street and hence the emplacements.

In our case, we had a pillbox behind an advertisement hoarding where there is now a petrol station at the foot of the hill, more or less opposite Wyvale Nursery. Inside was a six pounder gun from a merchant ship. We had to pull a string so that a flap in the poster hoarding opened and allowed the gun to show through and command the road under the bridge. However, one day someone asked what would happen if Jerry came round the side, so our Captain, who was an Engineer, said he would make a mobile carriage on which we could mount the gun and take it outside. When the day came to try this out we had to undo all the bolts on the concrete mounting and then, with block and tackle, lift the gun off its mounting and swing it over onto the trolley. When I left to join the army aged 18, after many practices on Sunday mornings the quickest we could manage to do this operation in was just over two hours. I hope they improved.

It was real *Dad's Army* stuff and we had a Sergeant who fitted exactly into this picture since he was in the Education Department of the County Council and was very proper. I was tolerated as 'the boy' and allowed off drills so that I could bicycle home for the weekend after the Saturday parade in the Brewery, which closed at lunchtime. I knew every hill in the twenty-two miles between Bury and Hadleigh. Having said this, everyone was immensely proud of being a Gunner and being ready should the balloon go up and I hope we would have served the country well.

## I Join the Army

When I was 18 I was able to join the army so in my Home Guard uniform I marched myself up to Gibraltar Barracks, Bury St Edmunds, complete with my Gunner badge to do my initial training.

Recruits were accommodated in one of hundreds of huts, the West Lines, which were installed alongside the Newmarket Road and we were given a good basic training, licked into shape to be capable of marching, saluting and all the discipline of early training. We slept on bales of straw in bunks and the huts were heated by a coal burner in the middle. There is just one incident that I remember from those days, when we were being instructed on how to direct fire onto an object. The Sergeant began

'In front haystack, half left, six o'clock enemy vehicle. Can you see it?'

And there was a young man there – real Suffolk – who said 'No. Can't see nuthin.'

It was repeated and 'No, still can't see nuthin.'

In exasperation the Sergeant said 'Can you see the haystack?'

'No.'

'Why can't you see it?'

'Don't know, Sergeant.'

'Well, what can you see, then?'

'I can see a straw stack.'

The Sergeant went berserk but to a Suffolk lad there was all the difference in the world and he wasn't trying to pull a leg, he was telling the truth.

My Gunner connections must have been noted because I was posted to the Royal Artillery where I was sent to learn radar and how to operate a set which could locate and define an incoming aircraft. I entered into this with enthusiasm and when I had finished the training, which I think I was rather good at, I went to my first regiment. Here, however, all my enthusiasm was diminished because I was only given the job of getting up early in the morning to start the generator to supply electricity to the camp and its equipment, which included the radar sets and predictors which drove the guns which I longed to use.

Somehow, though, my notes must have followed me on my way and I was selected to go to officer training and spent seven months at Llandrindod Wells in Powys where I learnt gunnery and general military affairs. By some miracle I passed out and spent several months at a firing camp in Aberaeron, on the coast to the south of Aberystwyth. We were teaching Americans to use the forty millimetre Bofors anti-aircraft guns. Every morning the plane would take off towing a drogue behind it and it was this drogue that was to be the target for the practice shoot. Now the only way to stop fire was to get the man on the gun to take his foot off the firing pedal but if you had to stop the fire in an emergency it was no good shouting 'stop' because the noise was so great. Instead you had to signal to pull the man's foot off the pedal. So a rope would be put around one foot of each of the men on the firing pedal and the safety officer or operative stood right behind them; if they saw the gun being laid on the aircraft rather than the drogue they pulled the rope and firing stopped. This was straightforward enough if the plane was flying across you, but if it approached head on there was, terrifyingly, only the narrowest of angles between the aircraft and its drogue...

I enjoyed the Americans because in the Officers' Mess they were the only people who talked to a young Second Lieutenant. Our own Lieutenants, Captains and above would just ignore you. When the Americans came it was like a breath of fresh air. All ranks talked to each other and a General in the USA Army would ask me

'Say, Lootenant, how do yer play shove ha'penny?' and he would be content to play with me and enjoy it.

My next appointment was with a light anti-aircraft battery operating in the South of England when the doodlebug crisis came. We were sent down to Kent to try to shoot them down. At first we were deployed near searchlight batteries but then it was realised the lights were unnecessary and the arrangement did not give us sufficient fire power intensity so a great number of guns was sent to the coast of Kent between Dungeness and Lydd and all along the coast to Rye.

Out at sea were Spitfires and Hurricanes shooting the doodlebugs down or tipping them over with their wings. The pilots knew very well the guns were on the land and that they should break off their engagements but some were over energetic and zealous and got shot down. It wasn't intended but unavoidable, because there was so much flack going on up in the air and the noise was fantastic and anything flying over was liable to be shot down. The idea was that after the Hurricanes and Spitfires had first go, as the doodlebugs crossed to the land, the gunners had the second shot. The target was a gunner's dream – constant height, constant speed and constant bearing; what more could you ask? All this was fed in and still we missed them. Some of the survivors went on to get tangled up in the line of barrage balloons behind us but I am afraid that too many did get through, cut out their engines and dropped on London. In those days if you heard a doodlebug and the engine suddenly stopped, you dived for cover.

After this came the V2 rocket which was too quick for either gun or fighter aircraft so we played no further role and I was posted to a static unit on the Thames Estuary. This had been there for many years and static summed up both its operation and the morale of the troops that were there.

## Into Africa

Finally I was drafted with several hundred other officers for overseas service and we assembled at a hotel in Marylebone which was the Report Centre. Every day a roll call was made by the Senior Officer, generally a Major, and every day the number of people in the room shrank with one person answering for several others. This was condoned on the understanding that if you were called in to be moved on, you would have to guarantee returning within a few hours. It was not possible for me to go home under these circumstances, however, and I duly reported every day. The only thing I can remember from this time was going one night to the theatre where a fine-looking man acting as commissionaire, with a row of medals on his chest, said to me

'Twelfth of Foot, sir,' to which I said

'What is?'

A look of horror came on his face and he said, with a telling hesitation,

'You are..., sir.'

I had been on a course in Scotland to convert from Gunner to Infantry and was wearing Suffolk Regimental collar dogs which he had noticed and which were those of the Twelfth of Foot. I have never forgotten this great ignorance on my part and the ex-soldier's expression of disbelief, as much to say: what are we commissioning these days? they don't even know which Regiment they are in. He was right, I didn't and it still rankles with me, even today seventy years later.

So the call came and we went by train to the Clyde where we embarked on an old passenger liner *The Princess of Wales*. A convoy was assembled there and after a week or two we slipped quietly away at night into the Atlantic. The next morning we saw the whole fleet of aircraft carriers, destroyers, corvettes and a range of civilian craft, carrying troops I suppose. We had German prisoners of war below deck but we never saw them. We headed out north west into an Atlantic gale and we still didn't know our destination. All I can say is that for two weeks I was sea sick and could only manage to stop being sick by holding onto the handrails and looking at the horizon, which was the only thing that was not moving.

Then with Newfoundland & Labrador in sight we turned south east, the whole convoy headed for Gibraltar, we could relax and I could manage some meals. In time we were in the calm waters and warmer climate of the Mediterranean, greeted by the sight of the Rock, its bare sides scored by goat paths and tracks, a right-angled triangle towering impressively against a blue sky. From there we sailed to the coast of Egypt and disembarked at Port Said, greeted by the insistent cries of the street vendors and an all-pervading smell I remembered from childhood at Bank House, when the men came to pump out the cess-pit. What happened to our prisoners I shall never know, but I guess they went down to East Africa.

After a couple of weeks or so we embarked again in an old Polish coaler. This was officially a 'dry ship' but for an agreed fee the barman could be readily persuaded to overcome this difficulty. We slept on deck, an operation which was sometimes more hazardous than might be expected. They used the coal from the bunkers on one side of the ship until they were practically empty, disturbing the balance so that the deck lurched over at an increasingly sharp angle. Eventually we got to Aden where we took on more coal. We threw nets over the side of the ship and small barges of coal came out with scores of people from Aden who packed the coal into sacks, scrambled up to the nets and tipped it into the bunkers.

After a time we got down to Mombasa. We knew we had reached our destination and were taken overnight on a train to Nairobi. From there we were taken out to a hutted camp on an escarpment six or seven miles outside the city. This was at night and when we woke up the next morning we could hardly believe our eyes. Looking out, we saw an enormous landscape below us with herds of buffalo and zebra and giraffe, like a very large zoo laid out in the wild. It was almost unbelievable.

The arrivals were interviewed by a panel of officers and I and a chap from Haverhill were told to report to a regiment of the Kings African Rifles situated in northern British Somaliland. We were told to make our own way there. This involved a land journey of several thousand miles on no more than a track through bush and desert. It took us a month to get to our unit by driving all day and resting at night; this we did in convoy because the local Somalis were unfriendly. They took pot shots at us but were never very good at aiming, so no harm was done.

I reported to my new commanding officer in the morning and he asked how much Swahili I knew.

'Just two words, sir.'

'You are no damn good to me. Go back to Nairobi and get yourself on a language course.'

So back I went another month's driving and asked about a language course and was told they would book me in but the courses took place every other month; one had just finished so I should return to my unit and come back in a month's time. I replied that that way I could spend the rest of the war just missing the next course. I had considerable difficulty in getting the authorities to agree for me to stay where I was and come back in a month's time. Luckily common sense prevailed and I had a great time in Nairobi in the Officers' Club.

Eventually I got on the language course and did rather well: Swahili is a very easy language to learn as there are no irregular verbs or inconsistencies. Back with my unit in Somaliland, I soon improved my fluency anyway since the only words in English that were used there were the military words of command, nothing else. For the next few months in the aftermath of the Italian campaign, in which Mussolini, who had tried to take over Abyssinia, had been booted out, we were guarding the supply depots which had been used to reinforce the troops. They were not to be used again yet it was their presence alone which kept me and so many other British soldiers in Africa as the war came to an end.

Our own askari, as the local soldiers were called, came from Tanzania and were a fine body of men. The only problem we had was that when you sent one home on leave he would take a month or so to get home, then take his leave and return to the unit. It might be three months before he arrived, and whether or not you got the right one back was another difficulty: if he sent his brother, you would have to start training all over again. The other problem was witchcraft, which was still rife amongst the troops. You had to do kit inspections without notice and look for clippings of hair or of fingernails, because these were the ingredients of a spell of possession. If you told someone you had put the spell on him and now owned a part of him, he would believe you. People had died as a consequence and so we tried to eradicate the practice.

After a year or so, now a Captain, I was posted to another regiment which was situated at Dar es Salaam in Tanzania. We were on the edge of a coconut grove and had very good accommodation in bungalows surrounded by avocado trees. The one I was in was next to that of the Colonel. Quite often at the weekends we young officers would go down to town for a meal and afterwards we would take rickshaws back, racing home in pairs, and generally the more you paid, the more chance you had of winning. Anyway one evening, after such a race, I got back and there was a tremendous argument going on inside the Colonel's bungalow. Eventually he came in and said

'Tickner, you are to put the Adjutant under close arrest and you will stay with him all day and he will move into your bungalow and meals will be sent down from the mess.'

I said 'Very good, sir. Can I ask what the charge is?'

'Yes,' he said. 'It is attempted buggery in a rickshaw!'

I then spent a very happy two or three weeks with the Adjutant in my care, swimming and playing tennis and generally loafing around. He was a very nice man and I am sure the story leading to his arrest was misplaced, occasioned by his lurching about in a drunken stupor. Anyway, that is my claim to fame. I shouldn't think many can claim to have put an Adjutant under arrest. I think the end of the story was that he was posted to another regiment, and I hope the record did not follow him.

At Dar es Salaam we were training to go to Burma where there was an East African Division but I am glad to say this was curtailed by the dropping of the atom bombs on the Japanese. Nothing else would have stopped them: they were absolutely mad on winning the war. That they lost saved countless lives. Many unfortunates were killed by the bombs but many thousands of American and British lives, including mine, were saved as a consequence.

With the war over both in Europe and in the Far East the British Army had to wind down and return home but this was easier said than done. Troops were still being sent out from the UK – Senior NCOs, Warrant Officers and Sergeants – to help run the East African troops. At one stage I was teaching Swahili to these newcomers in the certain knowledge they would be returning home in the short term, so I told them if they liked to learn a bit of Swahili they should sit in the front and if they didn't, sit at the back, read a book and keep quiet. Generally the split was about fifty/fifty so my pass rate was appalling but it didn't really matter.

Eventually, I got posted to the Divisional Staff where I became a Staff Captain and I had about thirty people working for me. I then discovered I had been made Sports Officer for the Division. This was spread over a number of countries including North and South Somaliland, Kenya, Uganda, Tanzania and what was then Northern Rhodesia. I couldn't imagine what I ought to be doing, so I asked one of the sergeants who looked elderly – he was, I suppose, about 35 years old – and he said

'Well, sir, you need a plan.'

'I know I need a plan,' I said to him, 'but what sort of plan?'

So we hatched up a plot before I presented myself, with some trepidation, at the Brigadier's door. I knocked on his door and went in and he asked me who I was and I told him my name and that I was his new Sport Officer.

'Very good, Tickner,' he said. 'What is your plan?'

'My plan, sir,' I replied,' is to make a reconnaissance of the major units in our Divisional area to assess their sporting requirements.'

He said that it was a very good idea and to go ahead with it. So with this assurance I set about organising a trip all around East Africa lasting about three months.

While the trip was taking shape I was looking forward to it but then my papers for release came through. I had been allowed out a year earlier than expected to go to University. I was sorely tempted to follow 'my plan' but it was not to be, and sense prevailed. I can only hope my successor was able to take it forward.

When the news came for my release I was in the unit in

Dar es Salaam and from there I took the train across Africa to the southern tip of Lake Victoria to Mwanza and waited for the old paddle boat which I boarded so that overnight we went the whole length of Lake Victoria northwards towards Entebbe near to Kampala, the capital of Uganda. Here I had to wait for a passage on the flying boat service to Cairo. There were regular thunderstorms over the lake every afternoon which was a dramatic sight. Eventually I got a passage with some civilians and flew up the Nile, putting in at Wadi Halfa and then Khartoum, where we spent the night, the next morning taking off from the Nile direct to Cairo. Then I took a passage on a boat to Toulouse in the South of France where I waited in a transit camp for a passage on the railway to the channel port. From there on the whole thing was organised in military style with stops at feeding places along the route at the right time for meals when they fed the whole trainload with mobile kitchens. And so came back to the UK many thousands of troops from the Near and Middle East. After some weeks, I was sent to a Discharge Centre where I was kitted out in civilian clothes and I was free after four years in the army. I felt a little lost but glad to be out.

# Chapter Six

# Developing a Career

### Back to Brewing

So after four years in the army, two of which I had spent in East Africa, I was out a year early in order to go to university with many others from the RAF and Royal Navy. There were about thirty of us ex-service men who joined the Brewing School in Birmingham for the three year course in the Science of Brewing under Professor Hopkins and Dr Cyril Rainbow. The first year was the most difficult in that we were doing Physics, Inorganic Chemistry and Bio-Chemistry. The work was well above the standard of what I had been doing when I left school with School Certificate. Some of the lectures I just didn't understand. I skipped them because they were meaningless to me and I got special tuition during the vacations to try to get up to standard. I was never comfortable with Physics which I found very difficult but I did manage to pass the examination and move on to a series of lectures on the Science of Brewing and Biochemistry and practical work on Microbiology, studying yeast and the spillage organisms which give rise to problems in beer, such as infections which cause acidity, cloudiness and suchlike. This work I enjoyed very much – it was rather like gardening on a miniature scale.

After gaining the Diploma of the Institute of Brewing in

1951, as one of the very few brewers ever to achieve a distinction in this award, I applied for various posts in the Brewing industry and eventually settled on a brewer's job at Truman's Brewery, Burton-on-Trent where I was under the careful guidance of John Penrose, who was second brewer. Then in 1953 my uncle decided to retire from Greene King in Bury St Edmunds whereupon the existing second brewer, the famous Octavius Harry Heyhoe, took his place and I was appointed second brewer in turn. This was not an easy time because I was bursting with new ideas from the Brewing School and from Burton-on-Trent and wanted to try them out whereas Harry wanted a quiet life before his retirement; in many cases I put into practice what I had learnt and told him afterwards, which seemed to satisfy him as long as it didn't go wrong.

At this time as a bachelor I lived firstly in digs on Angel Hill and later in an apartment in Sparhawk Street, Bury St Edmunds, in a house which had formerly been St Mary's Home for Unmarried Mothers. I have to say amongst my friends it now became known as St Bernard's Home for Unmarried Fathers.

Before it was customary to have apartments, 'young gentlemen' – that is young professionals such as dentists, solicitors, brewers, accountants and so forth – found digs, and a number of us stayed at what we called 'The Hodgery', an establishment managed by a Mrs Hodge who lived there with her mother and daughters. The mother was in the front room facing Angel Hill and all new entrants had to be interviewed by her to discover their social background and origins. One new entrant who was aware of this started a complete false trail and told the story that his father had fallen on hard times but had been caught out with some kind of financial swindle and had ended up in prison. So one by one we were called in to the  front room and each of us told that we must be very kind to Michael whose poor father was in Dartmoor and we all combined to keep the joke going. When Michael went on holiday with his family in Devon he sent a picture postcard of the prison with a cross on the front to mark the spot where his poor father was. We never disclosed the truth. There was no cruelty involved because Mrs Hodge's mother never knew; at least I hope she never did.

Back in the Brewery, in 1959 I became Head Brewer on the retirement of Harry Heyhoe and I began to be given pupils. One of the first was Peter Courage who came from Courage's Brewery and had been an Adjutant in the North Irish Horse – a reconnaissance regiment that was operating in front of the English Army in the desert during the North African and Italian campaigns. There Peter lost an eye from the effects of throwing a grenade into a German tank and as he was a very large man with a black eye patch he had a somewhat piratical appearance. While in the desert he had captured intact an Italian divisional vehicle called a Fornicatorum. This classical word translates in very human terms as 'a place for prostitutes' although in this case the occupants had fled. It seemed to us typically Italian to cater for every want.

Before the war Peter had been a pupil on the Elveden Estate and had worked on a farm in Icklingham where he was known in every pub. He had one gallon stone jars which he filled with draught beer and kept in the hedge so he could stop his tractor after so many circuits and have a good swig. One evening when he was with me in Bury he invited me to the Bell at Icklingham where he had used to sit with the locals. In those days the Bell was a real village inn and far from the gaze of visitors so that only the locals used it. There was no glass smaller than a pint, there was sawdust on the floor and the beer was drawn straight from the tap with the casks on the stillage where you sat. When we went in that evening conversation was cut like a knife: we were obviously intruders. After a while one or two other people drifted in and at last one of them took a second look at Peter and recognised this large buccaneer of a man as the youngster he had once known. After a third look he said to all and sundry

'If that ain't ol' Pete!'

The cat was out of the bag and everyone joined in the fun. Stories were told and retold about the old days before the war and we had the greatest difficulty extricating ourselves, though not before hearing several times about the time when one of Peter's uncles, a general in the army, came down to see him wearing a red band on his hat (which meant he was a Staff Officer). The story was immediately put about that he was a Military Policeman come to pick Peter up and take him away.

Teaching Peter to brew was an entertaining business. His day would start with coming in early to mash. He would then find some sacks in the Maltings and with a couple of quarts of beer inside him for his breakfast he would settle down to have a good sleep. Then he had to learn how to work out the brew which entailed some elementary arithmetic. He seemed to understand this but the first time he went solo I realised he had forgotten his times table – he was guessing. I had to get him one of those children's red exercise books which had the times tables printed on the back from which he could relearn them. Somehow he muddled through and eventually had a senior job in one of Courage's breweries which he ran well and where he was much loved. He found it difficult to fit in with corporate ways of doing things, however, and he returned to farming where he was a much happier man.

I had many pupils during my career at Greene King and we had a regular supply of Brewers from Whitbreads who liked to send a newly joined graduate to me to learn practical brewing before returning to the major brewery at Chiswell Street in

London. One of those was John Foster who came to me with a beard. I had to write three monthly reports about what the Whitbread pupils were doing and how they were progressing to Willie Lasman, the fire-eating Head Brewer at Chiswell Street. However, in John's case all he wanted to know was whether he had still got a beard, because in those days that was just about acceptable if you were in Marketing or Advertising or the newly emerging Computing department but not if you were a Brewer.

John showed no sign of removing his beard so when it was time for him to go back to Whitbreads I called him in and said he had to make up his mind what he was going to do about his beard because if he got well known as the man with the beard he would get labelled with this to his disadvantage. An interview panel reviewing applications for a medium/senior job and going through the list of interviewees, on hearing he was the one with the beard would ask who else they had got and he would get passed over. When John went back to Whitbreads he had no beard and I think that gave him the career he wanted. He came back to us in 1984 as Head Brewer and then when I retired as Production Director in 1986 took over from me, even though he had become convinced, as I was, that Greene King wanted to pack in brewing in favour of becoming a pub company. Fortunately, John and I were proved wrong and Greene King continue brewing to this day. I like to think that our joint resistance to the idea of the pub company played its part in the decision.

One other Whitbreads' story I like to tell is of how our maltster and chemist Freddie Reddish was head hunted by a brewery in Australia called Carlton who were most impressed with him and his newly developed pneumatic malting system which he had developed in the Maltings. Having lost him, we advertised for a replacement and the one we liked most of all was Michael Upperton who was working at Whitbreads. I remember meeting him on a Saturday morning in secret to interview him because in those days no one left Whitbreads and this was a very brave thing to attempt to do. I fear this was interpreted quite wrongly by Willie Lasman who said I ought to have contacted him before the interview, but this was impossible: it would have broken all faith with Michael because if I had turned him down and his application had leaked out he would have lost all possibility of further progress in Whitbreads. Well, Michael was appointed but at that time we had as a pupil Richard Martineau who was with us from Whitbreads and the son of its Managing Director and the story leaked back. As a consequence Willie Lasman and his second-in- command were dispatched to come and make peace with me. I received them both when they came and we talked about everything under the sun except the one thing we all knew we should be discussing. I thought they would never raise it and it was only as they were going out of the door, just before it shut, that Willie said

'All right about Upperton?'

I said 'Yes', but to this day I have no idea what he meant. We never got any more pupils from Whitbread.

Though it will be the only one I talk about here, that was not the only tricky moment in my career at Greene King, of course, especially when after 1964 I moved on from Head Brewer to become the Company's Production Director with responsibility for production, distribution and industrial relations. This was quite a heavy portfolio as Greene King at that time operated five breweries, at Bury St Edmunds, Cambridge, Biggleswade, Baldock and Furneux Pelham, while in the 1960s, as you might imagine, industrial relations took up much energy. Incidents could brew up overnight at any one of the five breweries and sundry depots under my wing.

Set against the difficult times, however, there were aspects of the job I really enjoyed. The people, of course, and especially the characters of the trade and their many stories. Then there was the creative side of brewing itself. The hop for me is the key to the recipe for a good beer and I became interested in the whole process of growing, drying and producing a good clean hop. I enjoyed travelling in Kent and Herefordshire to seek out growers of my favourite traditional hop Goldings and to research new varieties and I was asked to join the Brewers' Society Hop Committee, becoming in time its Chairman. Hops and trade characters came together every Autumn with my trip to the hop merchants in London. Until the early Seventies, all bar one of the merchants had their showrooms in Borough High Street in Southwark. Here was a chance to view the new season's hops but just as importantly to meet friends and talk, to discuss world politics, to catch up on the scandals of the brewing world, to enjoy a generous lunch. More than one buyer said goodbye at the merchant's door, only to be reminded to come back and actually look the hops he had acquired.

As Production Director I contributed to the production of a series of named ales through the 70s and 80s, among them a Jubilee Ale, a Royal Wedding Ale and the special brew for Graham Greene's 80th Birthday, which I mentioned earlier. These reflected a policy commitment by Greene King to the production of draught beer. It is this which I see as my major contribution to its development in my time.

It was in 1957 I set out to create a draught version of our Abbot Ale, which we were then just producing to sell in bottles and no more than two or three barrels of it a week. I got to know John Young of Youngs Brewery in Wandsworth, just as he was beginning to establish his reputation as a champion of draught, a reputation which was to see him described in a *Guardian* obituary, after his death in 2006, as 'revered as the father of the "real ale revolution", an iconoclast who believed in good traditional beer drunk in good traditional pubs'. I visited John many times and took great encouragement from his enthusiasm and advice at a time in the history of the trade when such cooperation was possible, without the threat of the company take-over hanging over our camaraderie.

John had joined the Ram Brewery having served with distinction as a fighter pilot on aircraft carriers during the war and after a brief career in shipping, so he had had no training and knew nothing of the technical side of brewing. This did not prevent him from holding strong opinions about ale, however, and his frequent disputes with John Rowley his Head Brewer, ringing through the Brewery in everyone's hearing, were legendary. And they always ended in one way, with the Chairman telling the Head Brewer 'You must go!' Whether he was being sent home for the day, summarily fired or consigned into outer darkness was never made clear and the Head Brewer always reported for work the next morning ... when all was calm, and it was if the great argument had never had taken place. Until the next time. This at least was the story circulating and retold in Rowley's obituary notice, but after reading the notice I rang John Young to ask just how true it was.

'I never said he must go,' he assured me. 'I always said he should go!'

As another insight into my relationship with John Young, it was not just where beer was concerned that he proved helpful, as on the occasion when a friend of mine, a dedicated fly fisherman, mentioned to me that he would like to try using a rare fly called a Tup's Indispensable. The reader may readily surmise what is indispensable to a tup, or ram, but may not be aware that it is from the tight fur which covers this essential equipment that the body of the fly is made. I happened to know that the Ram Brewery among other animals kept a resident ram, managed by the Brewery's Tup Master. Next time I visited John I raised the matter and he arranged that the Tup Master would go to work with the tweezers. I am pleased to say that this eyewatering operation was completely successful, several good flies were tied and in time several good trout were delivered to John Young at the brewery.

But to return to Abbot Ale. By changing and enriching the brewing process and using a finer hop I wanted to get a beer with a bitterness in marked contrast to the warm malt taste and, above all, with a hoppy smell that you would be aware of before the pint touched your lips. This was one of my experiments without the knowledge of the Head Brewer but it worked out to his and general satisfaction. We decided to enter the draught Abbot for the Brewers' Exhibition at Olympia and to our intense pleasure it won first prize. National recognition - and we hadn't sold a drop! Of course publicity was prepared and plans were made immediately to market it and Abbot Ale has never looked back since. At the 1968 Exhibition it was awarded first in class again and the International Brewers' Journal Challenge Cup as the best beer in the whole of the show. (*The Spectator's* City Diarist described it as 'a dark, strong, slightly sweet beer, rather on the lines of a bottled Whitbread'.) I think those two events really established Abbot as Greene King's own special beer and convinced management that real draught beer was the way to go. And I was thrilled that, on my retirement, in 1987, Greene King produced 'A BOT Ale', the label carrying my picture as well as the initials of Bernard Oliver Tickner.

Working for Greene King also provided opportunities for travel, not only in England for hop-buying, as I've shown, or when, as a Director, I had to take my turn on the train and accompany the Staff on their annual visit to Great Yarmouth with their families. I was also required to travel abroad for conferences with other Production Directors in places like Brussels, Madrid, Austria and Nice. As well as the chance to meet colleagues, with whom I was friendly without – now in a competitive world of take-overs and buy-outs – becoming too close, these trips provided opportunities for relaxation, getting my wife and me up many mountains for walking and skiing. For one such conference journey had proved particularly memorable, leading to my marriage in 1966.

Bessen Saethre (Bess) was Norwegian and we had met in the previous year in Norway. I had arranged a skiing holiday for myself before going onto a conference in Stockholm, with salmon fishing in southern Sweden planned afterwards. As it was late in the spring, I went to the most likely place in Norway for there still to be plenty of snow. This was a traditional Norwegian skiing centre on the railway line between Oslo and Bergen called Finse; in fact you could only get there by rail as there was no road to it. It was a wonderful old fashioned hotel, I remember, but I was disturbed on the morning after my arrival by the tremendous noise of young people going round the hotel singing and creating a din and eventually bursting into my room, bringing me coffee and cookies. My immediate reaction was that if it was going to be like that every morning I was going to move out somewhere more peaceful. Later, however, I learnt that it was the Norwegian National Day, 17th May, on which in 1814 Norway signed the constitution which led to its independence from Sweden. It is celebrated as 'Syttende Mai' with great marching and waving of national flags in the cities and all over Norway, even in its most remote parts.

Anyway, at dinner that night I was sitting with another man who was a fellow skier on his own and there were two girls on the next table whom we started to chat up, and that's how it all started. The next morning, as I was putting on my skis outside the hotel, I met Bess there and asked her if she would like to ski with me. I think she cursed because she thought I would hold her up but it turned out ok and I passed the test it seems: we were skiing on a glacier and had some wonderful days together. You could ski right down to the fjord where at that time of the year the apple blossom was all in bloom, a fabulous sight; then you simply took the train back up again to Finse.

After that I was distinctly interested and arranged to meet Bess in Oslo where she had an apartment on the outskirts. I am a little hazy as to what happened next but certainly a bonding was beginning and developing, so that in the following summer she came to England to see what this Englishman was bragging about and discover how much of what he claimed was true. The common bond involved outdoor walking, wild plants and a general love of nature, as well as skiing and a host of other things. So to cut a long story short we arranged to get married in Norway in Bergen.

I remember my mother came over for the ceremony which was performed in Norwegian. The parson said before the service that he knew the English had a habit of exchanging rings during the service and he would tell me when to do it. Well, he forgot so I had to take the initiative and when I thought it was a good moment I put the ring on Bess's finger; I think we got married satisfactorily. The next day we had to go to the Sorenskriver, a country judge with various administrative duties, including at the time those of our Registrar. We also registered our marriage at the British Embassy in Bergen. We had discussed where to go for our honeymoon and I suggested we spend it at Finse, where we had met. Only then did I discover that my mother had been skiing there in 1914, where she had been on familiar Christian name terms with members of the Norwegian Royal Family. Not only that but Bess's mother and father had also spent their honeymoon there and her brother. Was this just a striking chain of coincidences or was there some guiding hand?

All in all, I look back with pleasure on my career which I can sum up as an enjoyable and valued backdrop to what became increasingly absorbing to me, the pursuit of personal goals at home, in Fullers Mill Garden and in the natural world about me. Indeed with Bess beside me I came to regard the garden as my work and brewing as a paid holiday. So it is to the stories of Fullers Mill that we now turn.

# Chapter Seven

# Fullers Mill

### I find a house

In 1957 I was living in Sparhawk Street in Bury St Edmunds but I had always wanted to live in the country and in particular in a wild spot, preferably by water, and one summer's afternoon I drove out to West Stow, just outside the town, to look at a cottage in the grounds of the sewage works there. This was being used by the then Borough Surveyor George Standley and the Mayor of Bury John Knight as a place where the rough shoot could enjoy a picnic lunch. Previously it had been owned by a man called Thurston. He was the village carrier, and with his wagon and horses he would both fetch and carry goods mainly from Bury St Edmunds to West Stow. He also had some chickens for eggs and I think a pig or two and some sheep which he grazed on the heath so he eked out a rural existence there at a rural level. I knew the cottage would be run down but not to the extent that I found in practice and I knew then that it would be no good trying to renovate it as a place to live.

As I drove on into West Stow village on my way home, I remembered some people I had met at a dinner party, Roy and Tricia Wallace King, who had asked me to look them up if ever I came out that way so I enquired in the village and was directed down to Fullers Mill on the River Lark. As I drove down the track through the King's Forest with small fir trees which had just been planted on either side, I never expected that I would make the return journey having just bought the property which I was to live in for the next 60 years or so. When I got down to the house I was invited in to tea. The Wallace Kings had their small son Billy there and they asked what I was doing in West Stow. So I told them and they said if I was looking for somewhere to live why didn't I buy their cottage because they were just going to West Africa. Well, it seemed to have everything I wanted: the remoteness, the wonderful sound of water, the encompassing forest and all no more than six miles from the Brewery. We completed the deal over a cup of tea and I bought Fullers Mill at what was for me the outrageous cost of £1,500. Just when I thought we had finished, they said

'Oh, we have forgotten the island on the other side of the river.' (It wasn't really an island, rather a stretch of land extending from the mill pond at one end between the Lark and the parallel Culford Stream.)

I asked how much they wanted. I was told a further £50. I said that was rubbing the salt in a bit but I would pay it. So that is what I paid, £1,550, for a four bedroom lock keeper's cottage on the River Lark, with a small vegetable plot and an 'island', set in a poplar plantation on the southern edge of King's Forest, 2,500 hectares of Forestry Commission land extending north and west of West Stow village.

Fast forward to 11th June 2014 and who should come to visit the Garden but Billy and his mother Tricia, neither of whom I had seen since that day when I bought the house and garden. They had been in West Africa and lived in several other countries and never been back in the interim. I brought them inside the house and they were astonished at how it had developed.

## Building Works

When I first came to Fuller Mill, life was primitive: old black timbers, no carpets (in the sitting room it was bricks laid over a beaten earth floor), no curtains. There was a telephone, though, and I put in overnight storage heaters which were large bulky creatures full of bricks which were heated overnight. There was a well outside and, with a submersible pump, water was pumped up to a tank in the roof which served the kitchen and bathroom. After a bit, I did notice that when the river went up, so did the well and when it went down, the well did too. The obvious conclusion was a bit worrying, since I wasn't keen on drinking river water, but it seemed ok and it never crossed my mind that it would be really unsafe. I must have lived this way for half a dozen years or more.

But when Bess and I decided to get married, I drew up plans for an extension. Out went the stove in the fireplace and the two flues, one of which contained a mass of straw. In order to get rid of the straw the builders lit a fire and nearly set the building alight but fortunately they were able to pull the flaming mass out of the chimney onto the hearth, losing a certain amount of hair and eyebrow in doing so. Now at the end of the cottage where the chimney used to run outside, facing west, we made an extension to create a dining room. (In 2011 this was being used as the office where this text was being typed, with plans at the end of the year to create a permanent office in the extension of The Bothy, the reception area for garden visitors which had been built by the entrance gate. This shows how history keeps repeating itself, a useful illustration of the truth that there is nothing much new in this world.) But to continue with the story, the construction would provide a new bedroom for Bess and me above the dining room and there were various alterations in the kitchen, the larder, and the utility room with further improvements to the hall and front entrance door. This was all more or less ready for when we returned from our honeymoon to the newly expanded Fullers Mill, and you couldn't see the join. I had got the builders to remove the old black paint from the timbers – I suppose they had originally been painted black by Victorian owners, and I never understood why, as it looks so grim. The new joists were all from the Brewery, oak timber taken from disused beer vats. You can still see the dowel holes in the sides where the steel rods passed through to cramp them up to form the sides of the vat. Outside, the front plasterwork had all been removed, exposing the original stud work. This was comprised of pieces of oak that had been rough hewn and put up with leaves and all which presented an alarming sight of decay when exposed. However, one of the builders said we shouldn't have any fears. He brushed away some of the debris and took a nail and a hammer and, to my amazement, the nail failed to penetrate the stud and bent over double. The point he was making was that, hardened by a century or two of years, the oak was like steel. Now instead of the rough texture being used to accept a horsehair plaster the builders put expanded metal over the whole structure to accept a new plaster finish which is still there to this day. At the same time we put a boiler in a boiler house outside the kitchen and, with a crane, lifted in a beer tank which had been left in the nettles at Furneux Pelham, having been replaced at some stage and put there out of the way. This gave me a year's supply of heating oil for the house and hot water. I also no longer relied on the well for the water supply.

When plans were put forward to do away with the old sewerage works downstream and build a new one at Fornham, with yet another smaller one within half a mile designed for the villages around us, I thought it was time to make a change.

Luckily by now a water main was installed between the village of West Stow and the cottages owned by the borough to the north west at Wideham. It was just a question of digging a trench between the road and the house and laying an alkathene pipe. We were now on the mains for water, although not for sewage. With sewage works on either side of us it seemed a bit unfair not to be connected but the lie of the land did not allow for this. We still had to rely on our septic tank and I learnt to respect it for its organic ways and to keep the supply of cleaning fluids and chlorides down to a minimum – which has been a struggle with all the helpers in the house.

So when Bess came, things weren't quite so primitive. There were still no curtains or soft furnishings but we had an old oak dining table which had been in use at Hadleigh when we lived there. I remember my father saying he had found it in a derelict cottage where it had been used for washing up. I think he had bought it for five shillings and it has now got sentimental value for me. It is the table in the dining room now as I dictate this.

## Some History

The fulling mill which gave the cottage its name stood on the south bank of the river, between the river and the mill pond. There was a fulling mill on this site as long ago as 1458. The process of fulling was a method of making cloth thicker. This was done by passing the cloth through a series of wooden mallets which were driven by a water wheel, cleansing and straightening the fibres of the cloth so that it became thicker. It was then put out to dry on the flat piece of ground called a tentering ground secured by tenter hooks to prevent shrinkage. The fulling mills that I have seen in Crete and Norway are quite modest affairs; as they were only used occasionally there was no need for a large building or anything very substantial so I would imagine there have been many fulling mills erected on the same site here over the years. I guess the last one was in use up until the mid nineteenth century when fulling would have become an industrialised process.

My cottage was built for the fuller in about 1650 and became in later years part of the Cadogan Estate based at Culford Hall. The estate was sold in 1936 – I expect cottages like this one would go for £50 or £60 each – and the Hall was then made over to the Methodist School which is still there today. Incidentally there is another process in the making of some types of cloth in which after fulling the nap is raised or 'teased'. Fullers cultivated the wild teasel to produce a sub-species with stiff bracts and recurved spines, better adapted for the job in hand. This Fuller's Teasel (Dipsacus sativum subs. fullonum) grows today beside the Culford Stream.

### The Lark Navigation

When I arrived in 1958 the last of the old locks built at Fullers Mill by the Reverend Sir Thomas Gery Cullum in 1843 had been demolished and replaced by a fixed dam-board sluice, work which was completed by the Great Ouse River Board in 1956. The lock it replaced was sketched by Alfred Blundell, the Cavenham artist, in about the 1930s and from this he did an etching which we still have.

The navigation of the river was originated by the Lark Navigation Act of 1699 which enabled the creation of what I think amounted to 23 locks or staunches on the Lark from Bury St Edmunds to the point where the Lark joins the River Great Ouse between Littleport and Ely. The staunches were simply a single pair of gates so that a barge coming up-stream towards Bury would have to wait whilst the whole length of the river was flooded to enable it to proceed. It could be quite quick going in the opposite direction, between Bury and the Ouse, but during periods of low flow rates of the river, particularly in summer, it would be a very lengthy process indeed. Yet those were quite leisurely days and there was no particular hurry so it must have been a great shock for everyone when the railway first came to Bury in 1846 and goods could be sent to arrive overnight when hitherto they had taken months to appear.

The eighteenth and early nineteenth century had seen the heyday of the Lark and Lord Bristol now invested heavily in creating steam barges in an effort to speed things up. This ended in disaster, however, when a flood came down the Linnet from Ickworth after heavy rain, the dam burst at the Ickworth Park lake and the newly erected barge terminal at St Saviours Wharf (where Tescos stands today) was demolished. After the advent of the railway, trade on the Lark became less frequent and too expensive in time with the traditional exchange – of coal into Bury and corn out – failing. By the end of the century it had become economically impossible and the Lark Navigation finally was wound up.

There is a no doubt apocryphal story that, in order to avoid expensive dues, the Navigation Company passed the ownership of the river to an impecunious resident of Northgate Street in Bury, presenting him with £50 for his trouble.

## Some Geography: King's Forest

The Corsican pines planted between the road and the house came no more than half way up my leg in 1958, for the King's Forest was just over twenty years old when I arrived, and when we had gardeners who had been in the Forestry Commission – very often they lived in Crooked Chimney Row on the edge of West Stow village – they could tell us the names of the fields which existed around us before the planting took place. For example, fifty yards west of the turning to Fullers Mill, on the other side of the Icklingham Road, is a main avenue of oaks which must predate the forest, many years old. The field here was called 'the Frisican', although nobody seemed to know why. It may have been connected in some way with a medieval Franciscan Friary founded  on the edge of Bury. If you turned left several hundred yards up this oak avenue you reached Plumtree Lane, which would take you right through past the barn called Wideham until you came to Peartree Cottage on the far side of the Icknield Way. If you turned to the right from the Frisican you came to Mowgie's Belt, named after a small terrier who accidentally got shot in mistake for a fox. This would lead to a walk through the meadows to Wordwell. Bess and I used to go that way some times and even cross over the Elveden road, the B1106, and walk on to Culford Heath. There was an attempt to colonise this area as a village by the Reverend Benyon of Culford Hall, the Earl of Cadogan in mid-Victorian times, who built a school and a church there, together with quite a number of cottages. But you cannot impose a community on a landscape, it doesn't work, so the school and the church have now been converted into expensive housing. When I last visited, before the conversion, it seemed to be inhabited by characters who had some peculiarity or another. One would show you his tattoo marks from the German prison he was in and another tell you all about bringing in wine from his native Italy which he did with swear words liberally sprinkled to make points in his conversation.

Returning to the Frisican, continuing north on rising ground without having turned right or left, now on the left was Swamp Breck Broom, so named because every time the soil was disturbed up sprang numerous new plants of broom. It was well named. Further on, continuing up to the crest of the hill you came to Fire Tower Row and after a few hundred yards the Fire Tower itself. During the summer this used to be fully manned during daylight hours as a look out for smoke and at the first sign the alarm would be given. This was the theory but I don't think it ever happened in practice and the Tower has long since been demolished.

Turning left eventually would bring you to the Icknield Way and following that more or less to the crest and taking a left turn you would reach Lodge Farm Cottage, which the Dodgson family, very good friends of mine, rented from the Forestry Commission. They would come to us to collect drinking water because all they had there was the rain water which was collected in the well and they used that for washing up and personal use. As you walked towards the cottage the Forest loomed on the right and this we called the Russian Border because of its formidable aspect.

Looking at the forest as a whole, it was bought by the Forestry Commission from the Culford Estate in 1934, about 7,000 acres for around £4 per acre, and named King's Forest to commemorate the Silver Jubilee of King George V and Queen Mary. To further celebrate this, an avenue of beech trees was planted on the west side of the Forest and named the Queen's Avenue with a flint structure built at the northern end to mark where it began. As well as this, a plantation was created in the shape of a crown, more or less in the centre of the forest. I suppose this may be visible from the air but I have never seen it myself.

At the east edge of the forest was Forest Lodge, built for the forester in charge of King's. Over the years it had different occupants but the last Forest Manager to live there was Fred Jones, a fiery Welsh man whom I learnt about after many weeks of unsuccessfully trying to communicate with the Commission by letter over the state of the track down to the cottage. Eventually I received a reply saying that if the state of the track was unsatisfactory for me, I would have to repair it and that was perfectly ok with the Commission. When I told Mr Jones this, he said 'You haven't been writing to them, have you?'

I said I had.

'Never write to them, boyo; you will come off worst. How can I help?'

I told him and he said that he would come and repair the track, which he did on this and on several occasions subsequently. This was a lesson I have learnt: it never pays to write to the Forestry Commission. They are all very nice and friendly when you speak to them but get scared when you write to them and the answer is always the same – No! Mr Jones, however, was as good as his word. Incidentally, I learnt he kept Basenji dogs – the breed that are unable to bark. They are hunting dogs from the Congo which I had seen when I was in Africa; they can find game without disturbing it, being silent.

Soon after that I discovered from my solicitor that my

original right of way from the road to the house had been planted up by the Forestry Commission. With this good news I did write to them for once and that led to a transfer of the rights to the present track. At that time the land agent was Mr Reginald Snook, a rather lugubrious character who used to come to see me with a very small map and a very thick pencil, such that the mark on the map covered about half a mile on the ground. Once he arrived, looked at his map and said

'Mr Tickner, do you think you are encroaching on Forest Commission land? It would help me to know in which direction you are going to encroach next.'

I said I would certainly let him know before I did so, if it would help. This seemed to satisfy him so I began to make a small turning circle outside the house where there is a much larger one today. Yet on other visits when I wanted to buy land to extend into the forest, he would say I should have asked him last year or the year before and now they were not selling any. This used to go on until by chance I hit a year when they *were* selling and I then bought outright land on the west of the house which included our vegetable garden, for which I had up to then been paying, I think, £30 a year. This area was about a third of an acre but the first invoice I received had been for 300 acres, and, in spite of my pointing it out, this had continued for many years. So I had felt that I could garden quite legitimately as far as I could see. From now on, though, I continued to buy forest land as it came available to me. This was land which had been planted with poplars in order to produce matches, matches which with the coming of the Zippo and other cheap lighters after the war nobody wanted; the land was therefore no longer required by the Commission. Initially I bought an area covering the whole of the present Top Garden and then what we now call the Quandaries. In this last case the Commission had really no choice but to sell as I now owned all the land and the access surrounding it. Mr S had effectively 'snookered' himself.

One last favourite spot to mention. On the west side near the beginning of the Icknield Way was the Dale Pond. Dale is the Suffolk variant of deal, the term for the inexpensive wood cut from the pines that surrounded the pond. Here there was a slight valley which drained the light soil down to this low point. Although you would hardly recognise the change in the almost horizontal lie of the land, the fall was sufficient to create a seasonal pond which almost dried up in the summer time but in the winter or after snow melt would flood. Then the Dale Pond would overflow under the road and along the edge of the forest to the end of the Country Park and the water would go into the river where at the end there is a non-return flap valve to prevent flooding in the opposite direction.

To the east of the Dale Pond are some of the tallest pine trees in the forest where the heronry now is, although originally it was a lot further east when the Country Park was a rubbish tip the herons could feed from – now they have to exist mainly on frogs and toads. There are millions of these that swarm from the forest to return to the river or the lakes in the Spring and because they are liable to get crushed by traffic on the road volunteers have put a fence along the road to stop them crossing it. Once a day people are organised by the Suffolk Wildlife Trust to scoop them up in baskets from the fence and carry them over to the other side until the migration ceases.

### Helpers in the house
The first helper I had here before I got married was Ruth Jeffrey, Mrs Jeffrey, who was the wife of Bob at Wideham Cottage where there were four separate households: the Jeffreys, the Foremans, and two other families, all of whom worked on the

sewerage works on the other side of the road. I don't know how Ruth and Bob met but she had escaped from Austria to avoid the Nazis because she was Jewish, the daughter of a newspaper reporter who very sensibly got her out in time. Then I think she was employed in the Land Army, perhaps meeting Bob as a consequence. Anyway by the time I knew her she was speaking a mixture of strongly accented Viennese with many Suffolk dialect additions. Mrs J cycled here every morning except when it was snowing, when she loyally tramped through the snow and through the forest back gate into the garden, very often unwittingly driving several deer in front her. But when Bess came to join me, there were difficulties and slamming of doors. I seem to remember it was something to do with feeding the cat; I can't really remember what it was all about, but Mrs J had to go. Her husband Bob was a very good natured man and the butt of many jokes because of his funny ways. For some reason he used to bring the Sunday papers but how he got them was always to be a mystery and every week I had to show great surprise when he came. Then there was talk about the Christmas decorations he had on his cycle, summer and winter; they were never taken down but added to each year.

Sybil Fish was the next one to come in. She had been the village postwoman, cycling around the village delivering letters, although she was motorised by the time she came to us. Sybil was much loved as a real Suffolk country woman. She was very short and could be relied on to do any kind of job in the garden or house and was excellent at catching bantams. We used to get a surplus of cockerels which we sent off via Alice Ramsey who lived in the forest to the gamekeeper there. I don't know what he did with them – I expect he ate them. Once when we were visiting Sybil I asked her what all the pipes were in the field next to the house.

'Oh, she said. 'Them there pipes are interrogation pipes'! She had several other words we enjoyed, one of which was her version of the streptocarpus plants we grew; she used to look after them when we were away and her version was 'septocarcus'.

Anyway Sybil worked for us for a number of years until she wanted to give up her position because of ill health. She didn't tell me of this, however, and delayed her retirement until she had found someone she knew would be suitable for us, and she was right. It was 'wonderful Wendy', who then served a long time looking after us. I remember long discussions, some of which I may have recorded, with Wendy's marvellous Suffolk accent and her many interests: in archaeology and the collection of fossils, stones and flints; in wild flowers, birds and mammals, to say nothing of churches and ringing the bells. I remember going round with her at the Millennium where her band of ringers rang in the celebrations at Ingham, Timworth, Culford and finally West Stow.

## The River Gang

When I first came to Fullers Mill the River Gang consisted of a foreman and about six operators who were responsible for the banks of the river and the sluices. They were armed with scythes which they used with great skill to cut the vegetation and this was done on both sides of the river twice and either side of the Culford Stream too. As well as this they cut the weeds in the river itself. This was done by joining up a sufficient number of scythe blades to cover the width of the river and with ropes on either side they worked this contraption from down stream to upstream of the Mill. They also built a dam to prevent all the cuttings going too far; this consisted of branches of elder attached to a rope across the river and this held back the weed they were cutting as it floated down the stream. Having done

one stretch they racked the cut weed on to the banks in heaps to dry off and then moved up stream for another stretch. This was all conducted at a leisurely pace and it seemed to me that they enjoyed their work. I got their enduring cooperation by a stroke of real generosity, the simple tactic of a pint of beer all round whenever they came. They also knew that they could rely on me to allow them to have a good time off on the riverbank whenever it suited them. They could hear and see if there was anyone coming who needed them to spring into action. In the winter they made bonfires to keep themselves warm and to toast whatever they had brought for breakfast which was sometimes bloaters or kippers. They cut a forked stick to do the job.

After the great storm of 1987 we had many trees down here and for the forty or so that fell in the river the River Gang came equipped with chainsaws and winches and set about winching them out of the river and sawing them up. Any that fell in the garden they also cut up, on the grounds that in a flood they could be a danger to navigation. This was extremely helpful of them and I think they enjoyed it. I remember taking a video of them doing this work and what they particularly liked was when I wound it back: they would all be peering through the window at the television screen to watch all the trees going in the opposite direction and eventually standing upright on the ground.

At breakfast time some would bring their own food and all of the men, who came from around Sapiston, had wonderful Suffolk accents. One used to bring some food cooked by a lady in the village and he called it 'lugger-pugger' and got his leg pulled about it because he wouldn't say what it was. The days went by and eventually he had to come clean. It was cold fish and chips mixed up with treacle! The foreman used to tell complicated stories about different knots he knew and a host of other countryside tales which I wish I had recorded. Occasionally today the sons of some of these stalwarts come to visit the garden and one who came recently in the Summer of 2012 was a member of the Balaam family. Arthur lived in West Stow in a cottage two down from Nancy and Ken Curtis at Meadow Farm and he was known as Captain because he was the leader of the bell ringers and as such was Captain of the band. His brother lived opposite and was known as Pilot and this was because he used to drive the steam engine, or it might have been a little train, up the railway line taking clay from the bottom of the line up to the brickworks to make Culford bricks. The brickworks are still there but of course everything else has gone and Kiln Cottage, West Stow remains to remind us in name alone of its former use. But I do still have a brick with printed on it Culford Suffolk. This of course was the brickworks of the

© Ian Goodall 2015

*A rare visitor when Bernard first saw it (page 88), the long-tailed duck was seen on Lackford Lakes Reserve in 2015 and photographed in front of Bess's Hide, named for Bernard's wife.*

Culford Estate which enabled them to build many houses and cottages for their workers. The estate also had a dairy and was self sufficient in everything including bread from its bakery, and of course mutton and beef, so that it could live off home grown materials and food, all except tea and sugar. Alcohol was not represented in this diet I imagine because of the Methodist connections.

Today the River Gang is just two people and they no longer cut the river banks and they no longer cut the reed in the river. They will always appear if you send for them but they no longer have a pint of beer each and they are permanently on the telephone but they strive to do the best they can and do work taking boards out in the Autumn to reduce river levels for the winter and putting them back again for the summer time.

## The Year the River Froze

I had barely been five years at Fullers Mill – it was 1963 – when we had extremely cold weather in the winter and the temperature dropped like a stone. Every night when I came home from the Brewery I used to take the temperature of the water inside and every night it dropped until, at its the lowest level it reached one degree from freezing. This was the water from the well just outside the door, pumped up to the tank in the roof space. My colleagues in the Brewery who lived in the villages near Bury were in a worst state, however: because of the extreme cold the incoming pipes to their houses froze because the pipes were not buried deep enough. So every morning the good old Greene King fire engine used to take water out to their houses and pump it up to the tanks. Back at Fullers Mill, the river froze but it was just the top surface that iced up: the flow continued underneath and the water ran over the staunch to the lower level of the river. As the flow continued so the river dropped away from its icy sheath and near the staunch the ice became bowed and extremely unsafe.

Then one morning I noticed something in the river up stream at the bend so I walked up there to discover, to my surprise, that it was water. It had begun to thaw and gradually the cold gave up its grip although the mill pond was the last to remain as ice. During this period we had some unusual visitors. I was looking downstream out of the dining room window one day at what I thought were some gulls and then one of them dived. This made me reach for my binoculars. They were smews, beautiful little diving ducks, dazzling white with delicate black traceries, and I can't quite remember the occasion but during this period we had a long-tailed duck, another ocean going bird, again very beautiful with black, white and brown plumage. We have had other unusual visitors over the years, a ruddy duck, a wood duck and red-crested pochard, but we have never had such cold temperatures since those days, thank goodness.

## Foxgloves

Foxgloves can only manage to live in the meagre Breckland soil around the Mill if rain comes at the right time. Although there is some humus from decades of pine needles it is very thin and scarce. While the rosettes of foxgloves grow well in the autumn and winter, only if the rain comes at the right time to sustain the growth of the flower stem will they succeed and in some years they dwindle and only a few here and there manage to flower. But in the early summer of 2012 after a very dry period came the rains and we never had such an enormous blooming of foxgloves. There were thousands of them on the clear fell and all down the track to the house. Foxgloves galore; it was a marvellous sight.

It was Alice Ramsey who first distributed the foxglove seed

but alas never lived long enough to see the result and the great contribution she had made. Alice at the time lived in West Stow, more or less opposite Meadow Farm. She was a real country woman who had previously lived in the depths of the forest at the top of the Icknield Way in Lodge Farm Cottage where my friends Steven and Jane Dodgson used to have the house for holidays and then Steven's mother Mrs Clarke, who was a good botanist, lived there on her own.When she came to live in West Stow, Alice decided that to liven things up a bit it would be nice to try to grow foxgloves in the forest. In spite of the fact that the sandy soil was not really appropriate, she persisted and scattered seed in different areas of the forest including the track down to Fullers Mill. I suppose this was in about 1977. I was myself unaware of the blooming of the very first foxglove but George Brand the keeper, who had known the forest for many years, found it and took it to show to Mrs Clarke the botanist and he said he never seen anything like it before in all his life and was it a rare plant? She was very gentle with him and said 'Yes, it was,' but didn't add 'in this part of the world'. George was quietly proud having discovered this great rarity, as in fact it was, for foxgloves simply are not plants of the Brecks.

George lived in the village and was a very nice man whom everyone knew and respected. He could be seen with his gun to-ing and fro-ing from the forest to his house and always had his bicycle, on which the gun was slung. But George walked it everywhere; no one had ever seen him ride his bike. It was simply a machine to carry his gun.

Looking back, the early years at Fullers Mill were a delight with a labrador dog and two cats inherited from the previous owners. Bess and I used to go our walks in the forest in the winter time and when spring came, after supper, we used to walk up to the gate when nightjars were 'churring' at dusk and they would buzz us, flapping their wings over our heads to make a noise like clapping your hands, I suppose because we were close to their nests. There were nightingales, too, in the rough bushes near the garden, and in the daytime a grasshopper warbler sang its head off by a thorn bush near the stream. But today my hearing is not good enough to pick up its song anymore so I can only rely on others telling me how it makes a noise like a fishing reel going out.

# Chapter Eight

# Gravel Wars

### Finding Water

In my early years at Fullers Mill I relied on the well but decided to have a pipe put in from the water supply at the road before I married Bess and this has stood us in good stead in the house ever since. When the Water Company asked us to buy licences to sprinkle water from the supply on to the garden, we bought licences for several years; then they made us put in a meter at the gate so that all the water used was paid for and I soon realised that it was not practicable to continue like this. We bought a small submersible pump and one winter we got Mr Fuller from Ixworth to install water mains in the garden so that we could plug in smaller bore hoses from stand pipes so positioned that we could reach anywhere in the garden.

One day, however, someone I'd never seen before came down to the house and asked whether I knew that we were leaking water somewhere along the length. I asked how he knew this and he said he had been watching our meter. It was turning, and if I hadn't got anything running in the house, there was obviously a leak. So he put together a pair of small plastic holders with right angled wires which fitted loosely into them and set about divining where the water was leaking out. To my surprise he pinpointed the place exactly. I am a great sceptic over things the science of which I cannot understand so I asked whether I could have a go and he agreed. I held the holders with their bits of pipe and walked towards the pipe and suddenly the wires in the holders closed. I had to confess that I had divined the water but how I had done I did not know and still do not know to this day. I don't claim any special skills in this but I do wish I knew the science. This experiment enabled the water company to come and cut the pipe and put a new piece in where it leaked.

## Of Sewage

When I first arrived at the Mill the Borough Council had been responsible for the old sewage works at West Stow which was simply a succession of terraces onto which the effluent from Bury was pumped via a large pipe and a series of pumping stations to be spread on the top bed. The effluent would trickle down through successive terraces until it entered the river. This was a primitive form of treatment of effluent which was very successful in the days of low population in Bury but as population increased, it became was inadequate and in order to accept the next day's load 'old Bob,' who lived in the cottages opposite what is now the entrance to the Country Park, was told to go down to the terraces after he had had his tea and pull the plugs out. This he did very night to enable sufficient space to be made. As a result when the Environment Agency, or whoever they were called in those days, came to sample the effluent running into the river they found it was really of quite good quality but sampling the river itself downstream found the quality to be terrible and this was a conundrum which could never be solved.

It went on like this for years until it was decided it was no longer acceptable and brand new modern sewage works were created at Fornham St Genevieve and opened in 1962. All I know is that whenever I had visitors it seemed that it had been arranged to clean out the top beds of the terraces which created an appalling stench for a few days until it was quelled.

The large pipe which used to be used to bring Bury's effluent to be treated at West Stow is still visible running along the line of Scots Pine and oak trees to the north of the garden and the pump house still remains. It was as well constructed as all Victorian buildings are. I hope it will be put to some suitable use.

Nine years after the opening of the new sewage works, in 1971, there was an extension at Fornham and it was at this time that the West Suffolk County Planning Officer proposed the idea of a Country Park at West Stow for the people of Bury St Edmunds, using the land where the original works had been. This was to come into being in 1979. The old rubbish tip which the herons used to visit was landscaped and, once the gravel extraction which had started up in a big way around us in 1968 had finished within the Park area, a large pit was made into a fishing lake.

From the point of view of the fishermen who used it, this lake was not at first a great success. It was originally stocked with young trout, all of which were taken by otters. The trout were replaced by carp, of a greater size and living at a greater depth where they would be out of the otters' range. The otters simply waited until winter when everything in the lake slowed down. The carp then barely moved and became an easy target. Now when the fishermen caught their favourite fish, fine specimens which had been often caught before and put back in the water for another day, they would find pieces eaten out of them by the otters. Eventually the fishermen took my advice and fenced off the lake to protect their assets. The fence remains to this day, as in consequence do the carp.

## Gravel Wars

The first thing Bess and I heard about the possibility of a gravel pit near us was the news that Atlas Aggregates had applied for Planning Permission to excavate in the field opposite us in the low meadows between the Culford Stream and the wood known as Ash Carr. This was quite alarming and I spoke to our solicitors about it and they said the application had been turned down by the County Council but an appeal had been lodged and there would be a public enquiry to which we were invited. The only other objector was the County Council who at the enquiry had a very inexperienced young solicitor to represent it. The opening address was made by a Barrister, a QC, and he lasted all day so that evening Baseley Hales our solicitor telephoned me to say that we could fight this tooth and claw and we would have that satisfaction but we should be very unlikely to succeed. The alternative was to draw up a list of items we could say we needed to protect ourselves and to see whether the company would agree to them, in which case we would then withdraw. This was the moment when we had an opportunity to gain any advantage we could think of, so I discussed this with Bess who was all for fighting, but in the end agreed to the alternative. An adjournment was called by the civil servant conducting the enquiry, we discussed our terms of withdrawal with Atlas and they agreed to practically all of them. As a consequence we withdrew and gained the advantage of a fixed price of £50 an acre if we ever wanted to make a purchase on completion of the restoration of the land, and various other clauses which I can no longer remember. In my ignorance I thought that was the end of the matter, but it was only the beginning of thirty years of new applications every few years for a new lot of land. It turned out that having once been defeated the County Council accepted the gravel pit and its plant and would in future be inclined to accept any fresh application to concentrate the pit in one place rather than starting up somewhere else with a whole fresh load of objectors. Yes, in my ignorance I thought we would be clear after a few years but we had thirty years of it.

After I realised the implications I set about forming a group of people to represent the different parishes affected, which included West Stow, Lackford and Flempton, which we called the Lark Valley Gravel Group. In the meanwhile, I learnt about the long list of conditions that the County Council had imposed on the extractors, to all of which Atlas had agreed, in the certain knowledge that it would not comply with any of them unless it suited. I started to complain when they were doing things they were not allowed to do but nothing happened so I got in touch with their Managing Director, and when that didn't work I found his private address and rang him up on Saturday mornings. This began to work. After about two years he rang up one day and said that Atlas wanted to work the pit for longer than they were entitled to and would my wife and I like to go round the world at their expense for six months whilst this was happening. I realised then that I was beginning to have an effect on them and as the major objector I could hold them to ransom. I said that, no, I didn't want to go around the world, I was still a working man but what I did want was ... and I got a further set of concessions.

A large gravel pit had been turned into a sailing lake which was used by sailing dinghies in the summer but was shut down for the winter. The adjacent area was much shallower, having filled with silt following the  gravel washing process. This area, which became known as the Slough, I bought for the Suffolk Wildlife Trust in 1987 at the previously set £50 per acre. I was a member of the Trust and deeply interested in wild-life conservation and saw the opportunity to protect the wildlife habitats around us. I had realised that blackmail and extortion worked and continued to deploy these tactics throughout the tenure of Atlas over the years. I kept telling the Managing Director that he was fortunate in having just one major objector so he could afford to be generous with me.

In all this I had no direct practical support from Suffolk Wildlife Trust itself. Although it was already an organisation with county wide volunteer support, its only permanent officers were a Secretary, who was the County Council land agent Michael Lusby–Taylor, and a Chairman, a Brigadier whose name I cannot now remember. There was no Trust Office as such and no Director and its powers were limited. However, I always involved the Trust in my negotiations as I hoped one day it would take the land over. In response to every planning application I made it plain that after restoration the land should be made over to Wildlife Conservation as its primary aim to the exclusion of power boating and fishing. This approach was very successful and ensured that neither of these activities did take place, much to the annoyance of the fishermen who expected to be able to fish the lakes in numbers with umbrellas dotted all around, claiming that they would have no effect on wildlife. This was a failure to understand that the presence of human beings was not compatible with wildlife and their proximity had no beneficial attributes in spite of their much held belief to the contrary.

Once we had some land belonging to the Trust we managed to open the Lackford Lakes Reserve with our first hide. Bill Oddie performed the ceremony in November 1988.

But there was still much to do. By now I had extended the Lark Valley Gravel Group to include Culford because of the gravel lorry nuisance. We met regularly at Culford School and at every opportunity we could stirred up things in the press – I had a good ally in Susan Sollohub, then a reporter on the *East*

*Anglian Daily Times.* The next affair was the application to relocate a stream: to move the Culford Stream into a new bed and dig up the original bed for gravel. I discovered that a Research Scientist from Leicester University had been working on this for a year in order to justify the move, so I rang him up and asked him his opinion on whether or not it would succeed. He said it was experimental and no one knew, so with this I went

to the Environment Agency and put it to them that it was wrong to disturb a natural stream and also that the new course they were proposing was unlikely to prove successful. The light soil through which it ran - like the proposal as a whole - did not hold water. The Agency accepted this and refused to give their consent to the application. This was very good news for us.

97

The next application that was made was to dig up part of the wood opposite, Ash Carr, on the spurious ground that extra space was needed for another silt lagoon. I got various people to write in favour of Ash Carr including Max Walters, the Director of the Cambridge Botanic Garden. Atlas then appealed against the decision of the County which had turned the application down so that a public enquiry was held on the site with the inspector inviting objectors to be present whilst he familiarised himself with the proposal and the objections. Our case was based on the ecology of the site, saying that natural features should not be destroyed in order to obtain a short term gain of gravel and that their case for acquiring more room for silt was unsustainable when they had ample space in which to expand the existing lagoon. I am glad to say that this case was accepted by the inspector who turned the appeal down for the reasons we had given. This was an enormous achievement for a set of local rebels against a multi-national company who took the refusal very badly.

By now a Director of the Wildlife Trust had been appointed who was very interested in having the Reserve but feared upsetting the gravel company in case it changed its mind about supporting further development. I said this was taking risks with the enemy and I took the opposing view that we should continue to resist their applications. I now discovered that Atlas were actually importing gravel from another site in Norfolk to be processed in Lackford and I appealed against that but without success, because the county could not afford to resist them. We did succeed, however, when a gravel company at Cockfield proposed digging gravel there and processing it at the plant at Lackford.

Eventually there wasn't much left to dig at Lackford. I had always tried to be friendly with the people working on the site – hitting the top brass hard was my best policy – so I was now able to get the local staff to move land about to make walkways round the lakes which provided hidden approaches to the hides. It would have cost a lot of money for the Trust to have done this at a later date. Now with the gravel coming to an end discussions started with Atlas to try to agree terms on which the Trust could run the completed Reserve.

Initially we managed to get Atlas to agree to a peppercorn rent for, I think, fifty years, although we said this was not really a sufficiently long span if the Trust was to invest time and materials in the project, and over the next twelve months we managed to get them up to virtually no annual rental. I then remember the last meeting of the series at which we said that we hoped they realised that if they were left with the management of the site, at the end of, say, a hundred years would come a very expensive time for them. They asked why. Because, we said, in the meanwhile we would have put in elaborate and sophisticated means of controlling water levels through the system and it would be very expensive for Atlas to continue to operate and maintain these. They asked what we suggested and we said the cheapest thing for them to do was to give us the land now and they would have it as a living advertisement for the restoration of gravel pits for future planners to see. To our astonishment, they agreed and gave us the freehold of the two hundred odd acres of the reserve. We had also applied for a grant from their Land Fill tax which they could give us provided we found 10%. I said I would provide that and I think we got £300,000 for my £3,000 donation in order to build a Visitor Centre and to do landscaping works around the site. Our eastward extension was opened in 1993 with the Visitor Centre opening in 2002. This was an enormous achievement and the end of the story of gravel. There was no longer the noise of the plant or of the digging. The silence was deafening!

## The Trout Swindle

Round about 1970 the excavation of the first pit had been completed. This was immediately opposite the garden, between us and the far wood, Ash Carr. It had been excavated wet without pumping water out so there was a good deal of water in it already and after the restoration of the edges and of the meadow on the far side and the creation of a bund (a secondary enclosure to contain overflow) at the west end the water gradually filled the pit. This was purely ground water; there was no water arising from streams or ditches at all. It was just coming from the water table. After about a year we put in a small overflow pipe which twenty or so years later had to be enlarged to one of six inch diameter to avoid being choked with weed. Bess and I took to swimming from the boat jetty which had been built as part of the deal and we had many summers of swimming. You could feel when you went over a spring the difference in the temperature of the water. Bess was always braver than me – I think Norwegians will swim in anything where you don't have to break the surface of the water. She used to go out as far as an island in the middle of the lake. A line of pylons had originally crossed the land here and after the pit had filled up four islands were left where their bases had been. Before they could grass over, however, three of them were demolished by geese whose foraging made the land unstable until all but the one were swamped.

We also established a fishing syndicate, the Trout Swindle, thanks largely to Colonel George Browning of Weatherhill Farm at Icklingham. George drew up the rules which he said should be complex so that if ever we needed to get rid of someone we could always find a rule which banned them. This proved a pessimistic view, though, as over the years we have never needed to use George's trump card. When the lake was full, settled and clear we introduced trout which George explained could for the first and only time be small fish - four or five inches long - as once they had grown to nine or ten inches they would be capable of eating any smaller fish we added. So we stocked the lake with 500 small brown and rainbow trout on 25th January 1972; since then an annual stocking has generally been done in late March, early April when the water is warmer and more trout food is readily visible so there is no great shock on transferring from the fishery to our water.

We invited Orbel Oakes to join us for a start and then others came along, that is Jonnie Bridge and his sons Desmond and Timmo, both keen fishermen. So we had six people who belonged to what I called the Trout Swindle, all friends who paid their whack by contributing to the cost of the annual stocking, and the Swindle was simple … they paid, I didn't.

In the early years of stocking there was ample trout food in the water and good hatches of fly so that trout were coming out at two to three pounds and it wasn't until 26th May 1975 that Orbel Oakes landed a Rainbow weighing six and a half pounds, which is the largest fish landed to my knowledge. But two to three pounds is just the right size to cook and the fish are always delicious to eat. They look pink when they come out due to all the shrimp in the water, unlike trout from the fisheries which are pale and uninteresting. The pink from the chitin has no merit in itself but is an indicator of the good quality, natural food that the trout has grown on.

To end, a couple of fisherman's tales to do with Jonnie Bridge fishing with a tiny little fly at dusk. Jonnie was casting one evening and suddenly the line caught on something which dropped to his feet, fluttering. It was a bat. The bat had obviously gone for the fly and Jonnie had lassoed it! The fly had gone right round the bat without pricking it and he was able to release it with no harm done. The chances of this happening again must be one in a million.

On another occasion, when Bess and I and Gemma our dog were sitting on the bank Jonnie felt a sudden tug on his line and as it tightened it went streaming out and he thought he had caught a very large trout. It turned out, however, that he had caught Gemma, and Bess was almost in tears. But the solution is very simple: you simply push the hook right through the skin and cut the barb off. The hook then comes away easily with no harm done and Gemma was none the wiser. It was no more than being caught on a rose thorn to her.

The Swindle still continues and the names have changed over the years but the fishing remains good. Mike McNeil is now running the Swindle and always keeps me informed about the current membership.

### Otters

Coming further up to date, in the early summer of 2012, we were stocking the lake by getting trout from the aerated tank on the back of a lorry into big receptacles on the tractor trailer and taking them to the boat jetty. Here two strong men were carrying the containers down the slope to empty into the lake. I was standing at the top watching with my secretary Jenny when to our surprise an otter from the river came right in front of us carrying a fish, which wasn't a trout, in its mouth. Then we heard a noise from underneath the upturned dinghy on the jetty. It turned out the otter had stored her young under the dinghy whilst she went fishing. She got a shock when she saw us and went on out into the lake calling, with the young answering. Everyone wanted to lift the boat up to have a look but I didn't want the otters being disturbed so we removed ourselves as quickly as possible and only later lifted the dinghy and saw that there was a kind of small nest there. I suppose the otter had put her young there to protect them whilst she was fishing as they are vulnerable at an early age to a wide variety of predators. The next morning all was peace and quiet but as soon as I threw the corn in to feed the ducks they went in and out of the water as quickly as possible; this usually happens because otters are in the water around them and are not adverse to eating the odd duck.

The irony of the occasion was not lost on us and I hope the otter family has been grateful for all the trout we pour into the lake for its benefit! Larger trout are sufficiently strong swimmers for many to evade the attacks from the otter who is more likely to go for slower prey. However, I hope we all accept a degree of predation in that if we put food into the environment we must expect the inevitable consequence of its attraction to wildlife.

Otter cubs stay with their mother for two years or more. The cubs that were there on that day in 2012 had been born most probably in Alder Carr, the next damp woodland down stream between us and Lackford Bridge. This is a really wild wood only visited once a year by Suffolk Wildlife Trust to ensure there are no problems with water flow because this spot is where all the water from the Reserve lakes eventually goes into the River Lark. In 2012 there was evidence of another family of otters when a young otter with a damaged jaw was found on the Reserve near what has been named Bess's Hide. It was taken to the vet via the RSPCA, the jaw repaired and the animal cared for prior to it being returned to the wild. This animal was about a year older than the ones found under the jetty so either there are two families from the same pair in the neighbourhood or two separate families. Either conclusion must be good for wildlife in general and a positive postscript to the story of the Gravel Wars and the history of the Lackford Reserve.

## Fullers Mill Garden in 2017

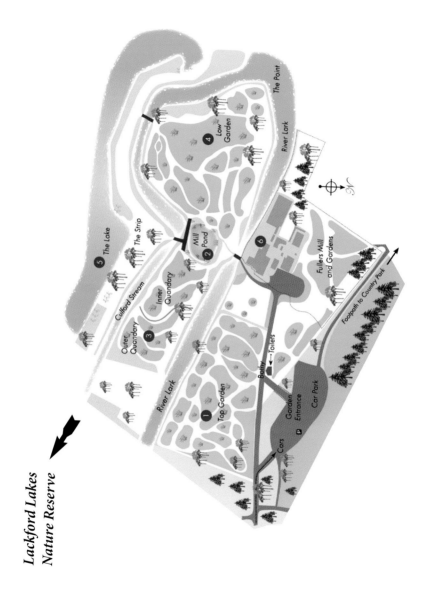

# Chapter Nine

# Shaping a Garden

When I first came to Fullers Mill in 1958 I had little or no knowledge of gardening. I was 34 years old. I had memories of long ago in the garden at Hadleigh where like most small boys, I suppose, I had been given a patch to play with, planting annuals mostly, but I had been four years in the Army, three years at University and three years brewing at Burton-on-Trent before returning to Bury St Edmunds and gardening had been only a remote possibility. Now suddenly, with my move to West Stow, it had become a reality.

When I came to live here there was no garden at all: Roy was a fire assessor and Tricia wasn't interested in gardening. There was a small poplar wood as you emerged from the newly planted fir trees along the track and then a little bit of rough land on the left as you came down to the house. So the first thing I tried to do was to improve the rough land and establish a lawn sweeping up to the river bank and in order to get the effect I had to seek lorry loads of soil to fill in the gap between the top of the riverbank and the lower lying land. The cheapest source of soil arose from the washings of sugar beet at the Sugar Factory and I suppose fifteen to twenty lorry loads came out to get the effect that you get today. This meant that load after load had to be spread and evened out and trodden, this being the best way of consolidating soil. All visitors had to do an hour's treading to help with this process which took more than a year to complete before I allowed any thought of a roller being used. Then the rest of the top surface had to be levelled and trodden, and levelled and trodden, until it was autumn and pretty well ready for seeding. Later that autumn the grass germinated. A simple statement. But even at this distance I can still feel the excitement I felt when I became aware of that wonderful first glimmer of green.

I was now master of a seeded lawn, a small piece of land behind the house, and the acre which I had bought for £50 as 'the island' and which was called the Lock Meadow in the deeds.

## The Island

The island was my first venture at planting. Surrounded by the river and the stream it had a high water table and I remembered that when we were young my grandfather had given my brother and me an island in the River Stour planted with Cricket Bat Willows, a fashionable crop at the time. We had eventually sold our island on but here was a chance to take the experiment further. I got Willows from a cricket bat enthusiast from Norfolk who supplied me with forty six feet high Salix caerulea which were planted at wide spacings, I would guess about five yards apart, in several lines.

I thought I could make a small fortune with these trees, selling them for cricket bats which demand a quick growth to give wide veins to improve the quality. The trees need an ample supply of water to be able to be make this quick growth but I don't think mine ever made the grade and by the time they had reached sufficient maturity to be considered for sale I had got interested in other forms of gardening; one by one they got removed until only an outer ring remains to be seen today. These create high shade which provides a dappled effect ideal for growing lilies and other plants. In fact we have now reached the stage, about fifty years later, when we are planting six foot high willows to replace the big ones which inevitably will need to be removed. The young ones will never actually catch up with the old but I hope will remain long after I have gone to create high shade for the future.

My original venture led me to get interested in willows and I started to collect them to grow as shrubs along the river bank and in the moist parts of the island. They came mainly from Hilliers but a specimen still in the Low Garden has a more celebrated provenance. Peter Balfour, then a director of the Scottish and Newcastle Brewery but in time its Chairman, vice-chairman of RBS and a distinguished Scottish businessman, visited me in the early sixties to discuss Harp Lager affairs. Knowing of my horticultural interests, he brought me a cutting from a tree I believe grew on the Balfour family estate at Balbirnie in Fife. It was known as the Napoleon Willow and was one of a number in this country said to have been propagated from a tree growing on Napoleon's grave on St Helena. Whips spread across the world during the cult of Napoleon which developed in the nineteenth century. So now the Emperor is remembered at Fullers Mill. I am still interested in the species including dwarf alpine varieties which I picked up in the Alps and Norway where whole mountain sides are carpeted with Salix herbacea. From a distance this looks just like turf and reindeer graze on it.

## The Vegetable Garden

I initially owned just a small piece of land behind the house to the west but quickly extended this by renting more from the Forestry Commission. It was one third of an acre in extent, although I have already described how I was regularly invoiced for 300 acres for my £30. Renting enabled me to start a vegetable garden and we set about trying to improve the ground with imported top soil. The first thing I planted, I think, was an asparagus bed and then the ordinary veg: potatoes, brussel sprouts and other brassica. Eventually we put up a fruit cage to grow red and white currants, raspberries and strawberries. We were told that it was best to have flexible netting over the top which could be removed at the end of the season and this avoided problems with wire netting as a permanency with heavy falls of snow breaking it. The idea was to keep blackbirds and thrushes from eating the fruit but somehow or another they managed to get in and without our help they could never get out.

For quite a few years we grew our own vegetables and soft fruit but then, with the supply of good vegetables and soft fruit at Sainsburys where we shopped, the enormous effort going into growing all this material became less attractive. This was especially so when you discovered you had either not grown enough or you had grown too much so that you were giving fruit and vegetables away. Reluctantly we gave up the fruit cage and the soft fruit though by then the annual placement of the netting had almost become grounds for divorce with all the shouting, 'Pull it back', 'Pull it this way'. It was a relief not to have to do it anymore. By then, too, Bess had developed an interest in dried flowers so the vegetable garden became a place for growing Helichrysum and the like and a dumping ground for plants we had been given or we were intending to move to other quarters. In effect it was a propagation area with an asparagus bed in it. The asparagus bed remained until we discovered we had a bad attack of Mare's Tail so I took advice on what to do and I was told to let the asparagus grow alongside the Equisetum and, perhaps earlier than normal, cut down the asparagus and then spray the weeds with Roundup. This I carried out and it worked extremely well and killed all the Equisetum but, alas, all the asparagus as well. What I should have done was to have cut the asparagus below the ground so that there was no possibility of any Roundup getting into it.

Since those days the Vegetable Garden has become even more a place for growing on plants, now to become saleable, so that there are lines of Irises and a range of perennial plants in rows there ready for potting. It is, however, still called the Vegetable Garden which is quite an affectionate way of recalling its past use.

## The Making of the Terraces

The next area I tried to garden in was the bank on top of the Island but this was very frustrating because every time we dug a hole to plant a tree or shrub we got out a barrow load of bricks and then had to dig another hole to bury them.

We discovered they had come from the demolition of the old lock wall on the south side. The men building the sluice had simply got rid of the bricks under the earth. This soon became an awful chore so one winter with the help of Alice Ramsey's husband, who was then our gardener, I set about taking all the bricks out of the bank, cleaning them up with a trowel and stacking them. I have a vision of Mr Ramsey standing in rubber boots in the flood with water up to his ankles; it didn't deter him and he continued working away there as if it was quite normal. I then sketched out a terrace using the bricks and I remember drawing out the design for this one Easter when Bess and I were staying at her family's old farm house in Norway, working in the evening by the light of a paraffin lamp.

Having drawn the plan, I then found some bricklayers, the two Barnet Brothers who were recommended to me, to build up three terraced beds to the ground level. The terrace is built on a batter that is sloping slightly inwards for each vertical face and on a curve. On either side there are steps (using paments I had secured from the Brewery builders' yard. I expect they had come from an old pub) to lead from the Low Garden to the top. It is still functioning today. It provided me with a good opportunity for growing alpines because it was very well drained. It did need moisture, however, so I laid out the then latest idea for underground watering, which was a 'leaky pipe'. This was formed by creating a porous walled pipe made from old rubber tyres which when connected to the water supply would gently ooze drops of water throughout its length and give the plants their requirement for water where it was needed, at the root. For the first few years this was ideal but gradually the pipe became impregnated with scale and I think I used it when I got consent to pump water from the river so I imagine the pipe also became choked with the organic matter in the water. The net result was

I had invented the 'non leaky pipe' and so far as I know there is nothing I can now do about it. In periods of drought we have to irrigate to keep the plants going. But was good whilst it lasted and plants that I brought back from the Alps, Norway and from Crete went into the terrace beds. They still contain quite a number of interesting plants such as Iris histrioidies 'Major' which has pretty well gone off the plants-for-sale list, peonies from the Alpes-Maritime which I suppose you could call Paeonia mascula, an arum from Crete, another peony which is P. clusii, a host of Galactites tomentosa (milk thistle) which seed about in profusion and a number of other plants such as Galtonia candicans and Saxifrage which need free draining and seem to relish these conditions.

## Steps and Paving

I was now having thoughts about the design of the garden between the house and the bridge with plans for paving and steps to the lower level of the river. I asked Greene King's engineering department if they knew of a source of paving slabs, preferably York Stone, and one afternoon a cockney dealer came to see me.

'You want some York Stone, guvnor?'

'Yes,' I replied and he asked how many tons I needed. I had no idea and I told him to keep bringing it until the builder said stop. 'But where will it come from?'

'Houses of Parliament, guvnor.'

'Hang on a minute. I don't want to end up in jail.'

'No,' he said. 'It all comes from Great West Minister Yard.'

So that is what we got: York Stone which had borne the feet of politicians through history laid by the builder to rest at Fullers Mill down to this day.

The terrace was built with shallow steps and treads down

**clockwise from top right:**

garden in 1990s;

Vi with cygnets 2003;

birch grove with Betula
'Silver Grace';

fritillaria pyrenaica
'Bernard Tickner'

[*photos Bernard Tickner*]

Lilium 'Lake Tulare'

[*photo Heather Medcraft*]

to a kind of landing stage at the lower level. This left the design of its sloping sides and I thought it would be a good idea to do this in flint, this being the local stone. I managed to get a supply of flint and then asked the builder to lay the flint along the sides. In the event he sent not one but two men to do the job and I immediately bet them a fiver I would be able to tell who had done which side, because you cannot get the same design from two people, you really need just one person to do it. Well, this put the men on their metal. They would lay a few courses and then go to the other side of the river to look at what each had done. By this means they came to understand my point but they were determined to win the fiver. It proved the best investment I had ever made and ensured a similar design of the flint work on both sides of the steps.

The arrangement worked fine for very many years and then one day, after a lot of rain and floods down the river, I looked out to discover that the steps were still there but there was a gaping hole underneath them, the size of a small room, where the earth had been eroded. I got in touch with the River Board, or it may have been the River Authority back then, and they came and found the source of the leakage with divers. They pumped in something like thirty tons of liquid cement to fill the hole and allowed it to seep through into where the leakage had occurred. Since then we have had several tests, the last lot done by the Environment Agency, using dye from the top of the river bank to check that there is no leakage occurring. Results have been positive, so I hope the repair work will prevail and save the steps for the future.

## Stones and Plates

At the East end of the house, there are a number of rounded granite stones laid out in a tapering design on the paving. These came one by one from the same beach in Cornwall that Bess and I used to visit every September for many years. Sometimes the large pile of stones would be covered in sand but in other years they would be exposed, the sand swirling around out at sea visible from the shore. We used to go down to the exposed pile and take our time selecting comparable stones in shape and size and grading them where they lay into categories such as A1, A2 and A3 in order to reach a final decision on which to take. Such was our degree of concentration that other visitors became interested and started doing the same thing. Anyway to carry the stones back to the car in a rucksack one by one was rather difficult. From the beach you had first of all to climb a steep cliff and then walk for about half an hour to where the car was by the Pendeen light near St Just. And the heaviest of the stones would have you over if you bent backwards. Our collecting went on stone by stone for eight or more years before we had enough and I think by that time it had become illegal.

The other feature of the paving is a number of gun metal filter plates from the mash tuns in the Brewery at Bury St Edmunds. The filters were made by casting and then finished by hand with the individual plates numbered so that when used in the mash tun they were always put in the right sequence to ensure a tight fit. Each plate had a number of fine slits cut into it to form the filter and allow the wort to drain through, leaving the spent grains on top.

After each brew the spent grains had to be dug out and washed into a reception tank in the Brewery Yard to await collection. The plates themselves were lifted and stacked against the side in the mash tun whilst they were hosed down, cleaning the plates and washing out the tun beneath them. They could then be restored to their original setting to await the next brew. All this involved quite a lot of manhandling and over time they became slightly dented and distorted, giving rise to unwanted leakage of wort which had not had the benefit of having been filtered through the fine slits of the plates.

I rather liked the idea of these plates and the ones outside the house are filters discarded as damaged from the Bury St Edmunds, Biggleswade, Cambridge, Baldock and Pelham breweries. (All those breweries now with the exception of Bury St Edmunds are shut – they were all alive during my day.) There are in fact many other filter plates around the beds in the garden and they arose in later years from me looking at the mash tun plates *in situ* in Bury and innocently asking the question 'Are they fitting properly? Do they need to be replaced?' And as one the work-force (looking forward to working with and cleaning their shining new replacements) shouted 'Yes, sir.' Then some of them would be shipped out here to make a mowing edge for a garden bed. We have had some visitors who have asked what they are, but mostly they arouse no interest. Nevertheless they have become a unique feature of this 'Brewer's Garden'.

## The Mill Pond

Nearly sixty years on  the precise sequence of events eludes me but the final element in landscaping the hub of the garden, which must have begun early on, was the reinstatement of the Mill Pond.

I remember stumbling across the pond one day, getting a wet foot as I came down from the bridge onto muddy land overgrown with brambles, fallen-down trees, scrub and goodness knows what else. This, I realised, must have been the Mill Pond. On one side was the stream from which what little water it still held seeped in and out. Above it, was a steep earth bank down from the Lark on which I had unsuccessfully tried to garden, as material either slipped down its sheer side or perished from drought on the free draining slope.

Defining and containing the Mill Pond took trial and error over many years. The first move was to strengthen the ground next to the stream to prevent it from running into the pond. The River Board then laid a pipe bringing water from the Lark and we controlled its flow with a valve supplied by Greene King engineers who stabilised the bankside, bricking and concreting around it. We could now control the flow, open up and get a good gush of water that restored the Mill Pond.

Once the pond was established I tried to grow water-lilies, planting them in tubs sunk into the mud, but I had no success. Far more successful was the common brandybottle, the native yellow water lily, a mass of which covered the pond and threatened to choke it. To get rid, I bombed them with a series of weedkillers, the granules wrapped with some gravel in a twist of loo paper and thrown out to sink in the middle of the pond. The method was not very successful, however, and I had to bring the dinghy round from the jetty, row out and spray off the offending plants. You can either have too many water-lilies or none at all and we settled for the latter.

The ongoing need was to contain the water in the pond and our attempts were now literally undermined by Pacifastacus leniusculus, the North American Crayfish which came up from the stream and burrowed into the pond bank. The holes it made were enlarged by the pressure of the water, which then as fast as it was pumped into the pond leaked out again. It was only after a career of reactive bricklaying by Peter Murrell that the pond wall was completed and the basin secured.

The Greene King Brewery made one other contribution to the landscape. The present bridge over the pond is only the most recent in an increasingly less rudimentary sequence of designs, but an original 'pier' remains. At my suggestion, a wine cask was sunk in the water and filled with concrete, forming a support at the centre of the bridge. The cask has long since disintegrated but the uniquely shaped pillar still bears our visitors' weight.

## The Top Garden

I have described in an earlier chapter how I bought the land that had been a poplar plantation, first acquiring a piece running down to the river, to your left as you approached the house. A lot of the trees were removed at that time and cleared for firewood but there was still standing timber and timber on the ground for which there was no obvious sale and I had great difficulty getting rid of it all. I did find a merchant in Brandon who took some for converting into non-returnable pallets suitable for sending heavy engineering parts overseas. I remember the daughter of our plumber helping to clear what was left and we had bonfires lasting weeks if not months around the smouldering remains of tree stumps. Eventually, however, the land was cleared and here was an opportunity to lay out beds and to start a garden between the track and the river. This went much against Bess's wishes as she felt that I had got more than enough work to do to keep the existing garden going without any extra. She called what we now call the Top Garden the Forbidden Garden, which would have been a very good title for this book. I fear it did not stop me, though, and instead I began to sketch out paths in the area which in turn created beds.

I did this not on paper but with the little lawn tractor I had. All I did was mow some paths and then see whether I was left with both a coherent route around the garden and manageable beds. I wanted, too, to create vistas in the garden, to lead the visitor gently from one area to another by enticing them around the corner to see what was growing there and lift their eyes further up and on. I kept altering the design until I was more or less happy with it and then got a machine in to do the cultivation: it saved a lot of work in digging. I then decided which of the beds I would cover with Fibretex. This was a fabric I saw the builders using when they repaired part of the track in the garden. It was laid in order to prevent the development of potholes and I borrowed and applied the idea long before weed suppressant fabrics were available in every garden centre. Of course in my case I was looking primarily to conserve the moisture in the soil with weed suppressing a beneficial side-effect. The builders supplied me with the Fibretex in large rolls so we laid them over the bed as one would a carpet in a room and dug them in at the ends. It is no job for a windy day and I can remember our then gardener Cecil Heyhoe and I trying to restrain the carpet as it was trying to take off. Having finally tamed it, we covered it with bark chippings and from then on every plant had to have a hole cut in the carpet before it could be planted. In all the years the fabric has been there, it doesn't seem ever to have deteriorated and I think this success depends on it being hidden from the sun so UV rays do not penetrate.

Most of the beds in the top garden have this Fibretex but the ones nearest to the present lawn and the river bank do not have it. This is because I recognised that these beds were potentially the best ones for growing lilies: there was more moisture at this lower level and provided I increased the humus content the beds should become ideal, by that I mean free draining and moist. Both these features are desirable for growing lilies and at first sight they are impossible to achieve in that free draining soil is seldom moist. But the conditions can be provided if sufficient humus is dug in to maintain the moisture level and the soil is topped with a surface mulch to prevent water evaporating. This was the policy for the lily beds which you can't achieve if you then cover them with a plastic sheet.

## The Quandaries and beyond

By the end of the 1980s almost three quarters of the present garden had been shaped and planted, all but the Strip beyond the Culford Stream (to be addressed in the new Millennium) and the last parcel of redundant poplar plantation now released by the Forestry Commission, between the Lark and the stream and to the left of the Mill Pond as you look from the bridge. Most of the poplars there had been felled but several I retained. In retrospect I wish I had got rid of them all because the sprinkling which we still have are now extremely costly to remove. They tower in the landscape and look quite attractive but they are bound to come down and we want to forestall as many Health and Safety issues as we can.

Once it had been cleared and dug over I had high hopes of this stretch of land which quite unusually fell between a river running above it and a stream below. I anticipated a high water table and an opportunity for plants which required more moisture than our Breckland soil usually held. In this I was disappointed. Any water lay deeper than the roots of herbaceous plants and we had as usual to mulch to conserve moisture. Only on the banks of the stream could we establish the primulas and coloured willows that are there now. Otherwise the planting is of familiar material – lilies, euphorbia and the like, spring bulbs, a few grasses and plants benefiting from the most open and sunniest part of Fullers Mill. After the place became recognisable as a bit of a garden I got David Downie, the local coppicer and hurdle-maker, to put a split-hazel fence down, marking the extremity of our work, and Bess and I tried like anything to think of a suitable name. We couldn't do so. We found indeed that we were in a bit of a quandary – so the Quandary we called it. When I then began to garden on the other side of the hazel fence we found ourselves with the Inner and Outer Quandaries and there is yet one more area, beyond a wire fence stretching to the apex of the land. This rough area remains in its original state, inviolate against my gardening proclivities, and is for others to sort out. As such it is known as the Trustees' Quandary.

The making of the garden hasn't stopped there, however. Land over Culford Stream is now being developed. It is rather open and exposed for Fullers Mill and the ground is flat but there is a solution for that problem. The inspiration comes from Beth Chatto, who in her planting at Elmstead Market so often applies the flower-arranger's principle of the triangle – a tall subject and the eye led down to lower planting. You will see it here in the established Beth Chatto Bed (the first you reach after crossing the stream), and developing in the second area under cultivation which we call 'The Patch'. In each case, the tall subject is a stand-out plant in more ways than one: in the Chatto Bed, a specimen of Betula utilis var. occidentalis 'Buddha' which is a graft from a tree in the Mount Everest Forest Park and, among the dipelta and romneya on the Patch, a Valonia Oak, Quercus macrolepis, growing from an acorn collected in Crete (though this in truth has some way still to grow).

Other projects will surely be developed in the years to come across all seven acres of Fullers Mill Garden, guided I hope by

## The Founding Principles

People sometimes ask me who designed the garden and I reply

'No one. What you see has just happened; it has evolved.'

For example, the layout of the top garden was more or less defined by the boundaries, with the fence being its limit at the east end, the track coming down from the road confining it on the north side and the river on the south side, and it was natural to have beds on these boundaries and around the three oak trees, two hundred or more years old. All I did, as I have described, was to go round with the garden tractor roughly laying out paths and beds that fitted into this area. Yes, one could say that throughout the garden the geography more or less defined where the paths and beds were to go.

When I began to plant at first I would lay out a bed on paper and put plants in at their 'correct' spacing and heights, making conscious decisions not according to my limited experience at that time (all the more limited in that I am red/green colour blind) but on what I read in books. Much as I tried, however, I soon discovered that what I planted bore little relationship to what I had put down; it simply didn't work out. I then came to realise that what interested me the most, and still does to this day, is the effect of foliage in its infinite variety and combinations. It is the sculptural quality of plants that attracts me, their architecture. And because I had so much space I discovered it was more satisfactory never to complete the planting of a bed at once but rather to wait to see what happened architecturally as it were to just a few plants and then to build on the success one hoped to have achieved. We still use this method, letting a space develop organically, which overtime has been the most successful way of building the effect that I was seeking. This is unlike that of most big gardens that are formally planned and have a distinctive designed feel, whereas what I seek here is really a lack of design and a more natural feel to the garden.

Pursuing this stylistic goal I have always tried to do the minimum of hard landscaping – terraces, paths, steps and the like – and although we do have some they are required because of the geography, the gradation from one level to another, but the majority of the garden is soft landscaped by means either of grass paths or paths covered with bark chippings and outlined by ash poles which are always laid to create a curved outline and leads the eye onward to yet another part of the garden. The golden rule here is no straight lines anywhere. And there are no monuments or statues or garden ornaments in the garden at all: we keep them all out.

One other consideration: in this garden of seven acres there are a large number of different habitats of light, of shade, a mixture of both, of free drainage, of good loam and moist ground, and, of course, water. This enables us to take on a wide range of planting with plants of diverse requirement and this has been important to me – diversity of planting, always seeking to put the right plant in the right place where it will flourish, rather than in a place determined by a need for pattern and display.

The style goes back, I think, to my earliest upbringing when I was a small boy and, recognising my interest, my mother took me to the woods where primroses and wood anemones grew. It comes, too, from my interest in the conservation of wild plants in the community and their bio-diversity. After becoming active in the Suffolk Wildlife Trust I was put on the Conservation Committee, eventually becoming Vice Chairman. We visited one by one all the reserves in Suffolk, reviewing and amending their conservation programmes which I could see differed wildly according to habitat. Not surprisingly this experience influenced the way I gardened. Ultimately, it is the way in which plants grow in nature that I have tried to follow here. Seeing the plants in their original wild habitats has led me to make the garden in the way you see it today, the style set by my experience and that of Bess of the way in which plants grow in the wild in all their rich variety of climate and habitat. There is no formality of design in the wild. It is haphazard and yet it can be used creatively.

Now from this account of the present informality of Fullers Mill, you might expect that there would be a glimmer of hope for a garden designer looking to organise things here in the future but we have kept them all out so far and I have concluded that it should be not one person but various people who, after I have gone, should be involved in deciding what happens to different parts of the garden. Really it is quite a simple matter. When a part of the garden gets so over grown with plants and is in need of a 'refit' it can easily be done by spraying it out and starting again or taking out the plants you really want to save and destroying the others. As to who makes the choice of plants, it should be the people at the time who are running the garden. They know best what should go in and we do not need either a committee or a garden designer to decide that. My friend Beth Chatto is very firm about this. I talked to her about her own garden and she says you will never get any one person to understand and to continue the theme and it is no good seeking anyone. She is content to leave it to the people who work the garden to make the decisions and not to make any special arrangements and that seems to me to be very sound advice which I am pleased to follow. And by this means I hope there will be a change of direction, depending on who at the time is running the garden. The old ways should change and not just follow what I have done. If a garden doesn't change it dies. But above all, like Beth, I do not want a designer and like her I do not want any ornaments of any kind in the garden.

There is one further feature of the garden which I should like to address and which visitors often remark on and that is the peace and tranquillity of the garden. You hear no traffic noise and in spite of being only six miles from Bury St Edmunds coming here you do get a feeling of remoteness and wildness, partly caused by driving through a small part of the King's Forest. The initial impression is reinforced by the looseness of design of the garden and by the fact that more or less wherever you are in the garden you are conscious of water and of the noise water makes. There is the sound when the river goes over the sluice by the house. (It is something to which I am so accustomed that I hardly notice it except when I go away, and then I notice the lack of it.) Then there is the spillway between the river and the pond and finally the two sluices at the exit of the pond into the stream. All of these contribute to the variety of water sounds, depending on the flow at the time but taken all together certainly making a major contribution to the peace and solitude of the garden. And it is important to recognise that too many people visiting the garden could destroy this very peace and calm which so many people enjoy. Therefore I would make it a matter of principle not to overdo the numbers of people visiting the garden at any one time, so as not to destroy the thing which you seek to conserve.

Now with the outlines of the garden established and having reviewed the principles on which it was built, and which I believe should sustain it in the future, it is time to look more closely at some of the plants and some of the people that have played their parts within it over the years.

# Chapter Ten

# People and Plants

### Gardeners at Fullers Mill

The very first of the gardeners was a retired tramp called Aaron Broom who took a bus from Bury to Flempton and then walked down the river bank once a week to the garden. Roy and Tricia Wallace King had said that if I put a fiver in the wheelbarrow he would do some gardening for me. I did exactly as instructed week after week. The fiver disappeared regularly but, apart from the remains of a small fire where I suppose Broom had made himself a cup of tea, of work done I could see no sign. So I left him a note asking him to do some digging, because I wanted to establish a lawn. I wasn't sure of an answer, not expecting he could either read or write, but to my surprise, I got a reply: 'autumn time for digging see you later on.'

And that was the last I heard of him.

There have been many more effective gardeners since, the next arriving as a result of an advertisement I put in the *East Anglian Daily Times*. In fact the only answer I had was from Stanley Bailey who lived at Lackford and already knew me because he used to wait at table at The Willows when the Holdens, who owned the farm which was where the Lackford Lakes Wildlife Reserve now is, invited me there for lunch.

Stanley was born in the village of Ousden, near Newmarket,

and was taken on as back house boy probably at Ousden Hall where his father was the blacksmith. Amongst his earliest work was mowing the lawn at the Hall using a pony with leather shoes strapped to his hooves to pull the lawnmower. Stanley progressed through the grades, and having successfully cleaned all the shoes and brought in the wood for the fires he became footman and eventually Butler. By this time he had married Janet, who was the parlourmaid, and the pair had considerable responsibility, having to go up for the London season where the family took a house in Portman Square. Stanley and Janet would take on staff on their own initiative to run the house for the season; then it would be shut down in the spring and they would return to Suffolk. This round of work went on year after year until Stanley and Janet eventually retired to Lackford.

Having been a butler Stanley was always very polite, called me 'sir' and used to keep in touch with all the nobility by reading *The Times* newspaper as well as the EADT. He would say

'Did you see the second son of Lord Falmouth has got married to Lady so and so?' and I would reply

'Never! You amaze me.' Stanley seemed to know them all.

When he first came here I remember Bess said to him

'Stanley, I call you Stanley, so you must call me Bess.'

And back came the immediate reply 'Very well, madam.'

He just couldn't do it. Stanley had learnt from many hard years it was always best to agree with everything he was told, and whatever it was you told him he agreed with. His philosophy was that it was much quicker to agree and save a lot of argument. Some things, however, he couldn't quite manage.

Stanley had many years in the garden here, I think working two days a week. After he had retired completely, ceasing his employment at The Willows, the family gave him and Janet a nice bungalow at the end of the garden. In those days people looked after their staff in their employ and in their retirement.

When Bess and I went away on a bank holiday, Stanley and sometimes Janet used to look after the house and garden; they used to spend quite a lot of the time 'guarding' the place. We know this because friends told us that when they came Stanley would very politely ask 'Are you a friend of Mr Tickner, sir?' and only those who passed the test could come in; maybe he learnt to do this from his son who was a policeman. Anyway, Stanley regularly borrowed Bess's car so that he could drive here to feed the cats and birds everyday whilst we were away. When he became rather elderly I thought I had better test his driving so one year I asked whether he would drive me around a bit. It was fairly terrifying so I said to him

'Stanley, I don't think you should drive into Bury.'

He immediately said 'Very good, sir,' as usual, so I was quite confident he wouldn't do it.

When we got back from holiday he said to me in a reassuring way

'I got on all right with the driving, sir.'

'Oh,' I said. 'Good, Stanley. I am very glad to hear it.'

'I didn't go to Bury,' he said.

'Good.'

'I went to Sudbury instead'!

Eventually one day, when attempting to drive into the County Club in Looms Lane to park, Stanley indicated left and took a wide sweep to the right – to let the horse see the opening (having been brought up to drive a horse and trap) and of course the following car bumped straight into him. He told me later that he got out and asked the driver whether he knew who owned my car. The man said not, so Stanley told him that it belonged to Mr Tickner.

'That's all we want,' said the driver. He was no friend of mine.

After this Stanley himself decided to retire from driving, either to Bury or to Sudbury.

When he became rather infirm we got him into Risby Hall nursing home and I and his niece who lived at Ousden paid for him with contributions from his son and the Holdens. I then hit on the idea of speaking to his old regiment because Stanley had been wounded at the Battle of the Somme in the 1914-18 war. I got in touch with them and sent Stanley's army number and to my amazement they had his full details and agreed to help with the finances. This went on until his death and the regiment still supported Janet when she went into the nursing home and with our help remained there.

Many of the gardeners who worked at Fullers Mill were men from the Forestry Commission, retired and living close by in West Stow village, often on Crooked Chimney Row. This was so called because the chimneys were shaped in a dog leg fashion, although you can no longer see the crook since the Forestry Commission enclosed the chimneys within the houses when providing the properties with bathrooms at the back. Among the stalwarts of Crooked Chimney Row was Cecil Heyhoe.

Cecil was from a local family: he had relations in Lackford and a brother who had been in the Guards and worked for the Brewery long after his retirement date. Cecil himself ran a milk delivery service for many years after he had retired from the Forestry Commission. He left a pint of milk every day at our gate bringing it very early in the morning, often in the dark. All went ok except on one occasion. I had got too much milk and left a note for him in the tub which said 'No more milk until Thursday.' Well, the the milk kept coming, next day and the day after. The note had gone, so I knew that Cecil was aware of what I wanted. I went to see him (he lived in the first cottage in the row) and the conversation went like this:

'I put a note in for you, Cecil,' I said.

'Yes,' he said. 'Got your note all right.'

'I am still getting a pint of milk everyday.

'Yes,' he said. 'A pint of milk everyday. Putting it there regular.'

I could not understand this so I tried again.

'But, Cecil, I put a note in there.'

'Yes, I know you did. I got your note all right. But that was too dark to read it.'

The years went by and suddenly I was getting no milk at all, not a single pint, so I went to see Cecil again.

'Cecil, I am not getting any milk.'

'Well that's a rum en,' he said.' I putten on it in.'

'Well, I reckon someone's taken it out.'

'Yes,' Cecil came back. 'There's a man in the Forestry, he's been having a pint everyday as regular but the last few days he 'hint of bin haven' none. I reckon he's haven' your milk.'

I rang up the local bobby PC Moss who lived at Ingham

and bicycled slowly around the countryside on a big standup and beg bicycle. He listened to my story very carefully.

'Beggin' your pardon, sir,' he said (he had a deep bassed voice like the policeman in *Toy Town*), 'but do you think it was human beings which took your milk?' He said he knew of an alsatian dog who had taken thirty pints of milk off someone's doorstep but I told him that I had a tub with a lid on it and he said

'Leave that to me, sir.'

A few mornings later I was going into the Brewery early, around 6am, so I stopped at the gate to look and see if there was any milk. I lifted the lid of the tub and PC Moss sprung up from the heather nearby and looked at me very accusingly and I in turn felt extremely guilty. Having got over this little local difficulty, the policeman settled himself down again (he must have left his bicycle out of sight somewhere) so I said

'What shall I do? Shall I put the milk back?'

'Yes,' he said. 'Put that back. There is plenty of time to catch them yet.'

I went off to the Brewery and when I got home I telephoned PC Moss and asked if he had caught anyone.

'You won't have no more trouble, sir,' he said.

'Well, who's doing it?'

'You'll be all right now, sir,' he replied. He wouldn't say any more, but I expect he warned them off good and proper.

Cecil Heyhoe was always a meticulous gardener. An area he was given to work, on completion would be perfect. There would not be a single weed or stone to be seen; it would be raked absolutely clean. I could never ween him off this way of working. What I, and indeed the garden, wanted was a wider spread gardened to a lower standard to keep things reasonably tidy. However, when we were working together on some new kind of work, which neither of us had encountered before, we would try various ways of doing it – some better than others – until we eventually found the way which really did work. Then Cecil would say

'Time we done this here, we'll know how to do it.' This summed up the situation very well and ensured success should we ever meet the same problem again.

Cecil was a perfectionist and like all perfectionists he was a worrier; he always had some deep seated worry. I think this was the main cause of pains he had in his stomach. He used to have terrible pains and he would go to see the doctor who could never trace anything wrong with him. I used to ask Cecil about his discussions and asked if he had told the doctor where it hurt.

'Oh no,' he used to say. 'I didn't tell him nothing like that.'

'Why?'

'Well,' he said, 'it's like this here. The doctor has got his job to do and I don't want to put him off on the wrong trail by telling him things he'd have to find out himself to be any good.'

He was adamant in this. He must have been the despair of all doctors. He would have been better off going to see the vet!

Reg Frost was a bachelor and lived in the second cottage on Crooked Chimney Row. He was known as quite a scholar because he was the *Bury Free Press* correspondent for the village. He would lie in wait for me to get a lift into Bury and would always be full of stories. But Reg was always spending too much money on the horses. He never had enough money to put in the slot machine for electricity so he asked Mr Curtis across at the farm to leave his yard light on so that he could see how to go to bed.

One day on one of his lifts in with me Reg seemed highly excited. The builders had come to renovate the row of cottages for the Forestry Commission and build on an extra amount at the back to create bathrooms for every property but the reason Reg was excited was that the builder had accused him of stealing the 'arco' and selling it. I asked what an arco was.

'Well there, I wish I know,' Reg said. 'I don't know what the arco is. I don't want to get on the wrong side of the builder. He's a relation of mine and if he found I had stolen the arco I would be in great trouble.'

The story kept running for several weeks and then came the conclusion.

'They found the arco.'

'Where was it?' I asked.

'They had hidden it under my bed. (The arco was the builder's acrow prop.) They kept saying I had stolen it, but that's where they found it.'

Another ex-Forestry Commission man was Sid Dorling who I think had worked all his life in the forest and he was a good steady man, utterly reliable. I remember him for helping me with some of those bricks we discovered which turned out to be the old lock wall. Sid continued to work in the garden for many years until eventually he got cancer. Sid himself wasn't told, nor was he taken into hospital, but Mrs Dorling knew and I knew and when I used to go to see him he would always be looking anxious and wanting to ask the question which was never put. In those days doctors were not confiding as they are now. It was sad to see him slowly dwindle.

### Friends and Influences

My first guides to gardening were met not in person but through their books. They included Marjorie Fish, who wrote of East Lambrook Manor that 'It is pleasant to know each one of your plants intimately because you have chosen and planted every one of them', and two writers I would describe as 'nicely opinionated'. I was to meet Christopher Lloyd and share opinions in person, but I came to know Graham Stuart Thomas through his writings, not so much his classic books on roses but more general works like *Perennial Garden Plants*. Perhaps Thomas should be seen as the presiding genius of Fullers Mill Garden. His insistence on the integrity of the species and his purist's distaste for modern hybrids made the link for me between my childhood delight in wild flowers and the idea of making a garden.

Turning now to people who have influenced me greatly in person, I suppose the earliest was Sir Cedric Morris at Hadleigh although, as I have described, in the early years of my youth his house and its occupants were strictly out of bounds. Later in life

I got to know him and share his enthusiasm for plants, especially for irises, although I have had many different plants from him which I treasure.

The next influence, I suppose, was Mary Barnard who gardened near Malvern. She was one of the first growers and hybridisers of hellebores. I used to buy a few from her every year in those days when they were named varieties. Eventually Bess and I went to see here on one of my visits to look at hops growing nearby and we enjoyed meeting her and her husband. I remember at the time we had a car full of plants, having visited several nurseries before we went to their garden, and we took several hybrids back from the Ballards' Old Court Nursery in Colwall. They included one which I know we still have, a very small dark coloured flower called 'Philip Ballard'. Since those days many new varieties have been hybridised by numerous growers so that named varieties aren't so frequent. Also at that time we used to visit Great Dixter where it was always a pleasure to meet Christopher Lloyd and buy some plants from him and then onto Washfield Nursery at Hawkhurst and select plants from Elizabeth Strangman. She grew plants in the old fashioned way in clay pots and these were plunged in sand and gravel beds so that moisture could be retained. When you bought a plant she simply knocked one out of the clay pot and rolled it up in newspaper to take home with not a plastic pot in sight. She also was one of the early hybridists of hellebores.

Other personalities must include the formidable Maybud Campbell whose stature denied her diminutive name. I had introductions to her from Max Walters at Cambridge Botanic Garden and Edgar Milne Redhead, a former senior manager at Kew. Maybud lived at Menton on the Côte d'Azur. Her father had a medical practice there amongst the English community who went there for the winter season. He looked after them with great skill and then returned for the summer to his home with Maybud at Layer Marney Hall near Colchester where they lived in considerable style. Meanwhile at Menton Dr Campbell developed a botanic garden and did quite a lot of work hybridising citrus fruits, many of which still survive commercially. Eventually he left the botanic garden to Menton and his daughter moved out to the gardener's cottage which overlooked the garden.

Maybud also kept an apartment in the town itself near the casino which she made available to generations of young gardeners from Kew and Cambridge Botanic and Bess and I were fortunate enough somehow to fall into this category. We went out during the day and reported back to our hostess by telephone when we got back in the evening, when we were told we had been to the wrong places and seen all the wrong plants! It was quite a daunting experience to meet up with Maybud who was extremely knowledgeable about the whole area and where plants were. On some days we went out with her, we in our hire car and she being driven by a night porter from one of the Riviera hotels. We visited colonies of plants we would never have found on our own. However, one day we went to a place where the ground fell off sharply from the road and on the lower levels there were a lot of peonies, I suppose P.mascula, and Miss Campbell said

'You can dig here, my dears, because a new road is going to come right through here and all this will be destroyed.'

So I went down below the road and started digging the smallest seedling I could find and its roots went down and down and down. Eventually I emerged in triumph above the road with the seedling, only to find an irate Frenchman who rounded on me severely, in English, for taking French plants away. At this, Maybud turned on her heel and walked off in the opposite direction and there was no talk of new roads and such. I had to take all the irate criticism. I felt the easiest thing to do was to follow Stanley Bailey's example and agree with everything he said – which I don't suppose the French are used to. It did stop fairly quickly after that.

Maybud always had several projects on the go. She continued to pursue the interest in the Outer Hebrides which had led to her earlier *Flora of Uig* (1945), visiting the islands and doing a lot of work with a young researcher. She was also involved in the *Flora Europaea* project and on one occasion enlisted my help. I was due to attend one of our European Brewers' Conferences in Helsinki, and afterwards Bess and I had arranged to travel the short distance to Leningrad to see the sights. Learning of this, Maybud asked me to look up the Russian contributor to the *Flora*, essentially to nudge him into action. Before the meeting I wrote to ask if there was anything I could bring from England for my contact, unavailable to him in Russia. As a result I found myself nervously negotiating customs with a bag of the Cold War spy stories popular at the time: John Le Carré, Len Deighton and the like! What I remember of the eventual meeting is travelling long corridors, doors ajar on either side, through a museum full of people where absolutely nothing was happening. The policy seemed to be to guarantee full employment, even when there was no work to be done. State sponsored sloth! My contact was no exception to the rule. He made an affable host across the samovar but I have no doubt he could have found plenty of time for *Flora Europaea*, had he been so inclined. His was the Garden of Idleness.

Maybud used to visit England every year to see her banker, broker and her many friends. She would be taken from the South of France by a variety of friends to reach the channel port which she then managed on her own. She travelled with copious luggage including all her bed linen, which she insisted should be washed separately and to her instructions wherever she went. In England she would again be handed from one friend to another, sometimes leaving luggage to be collected on the return trip. She used to come and stay with us here at Fullers Mill and I only wish I had recorded her many stories, some quite scurrilous, about notables of the day in the plant world. It poured

136

out of her and the only way to stop the flow was to go and get a weed from the garden and ask her to key it out (to identify the plant by working through pre-determined questions about its key features). This silenced her for quite some while.

On one occasion Bess took Maybud on by car to the Milne-Redheads, who lived in Nayland, and got thoroughly lost, only to be castigated by Maybud for not having a map in the car to find out where to go. By that time Edgar Redhead had retired from Kew and had become a force within the Suffolk Wildlife Trust. I went out on many expeditions with him which was well worth while because he knew so many people and he knew so many plants. In particular, it was he who inspired great interest in the reestablishment of the black poplar in the UK and he had a young man who was going to take this on after Edgar's death in 1996. I have a feeling this never actually took place but Edgar had done an enormous amount of work and the black poplar is now well and truly growing in many places in the countryside including the garden here. I went to Edgar's daughter and son-in-law's house just over the border into Essex when the Lord Lieutenant presented Edgar with his MBE from the Queen and I remember Edgar thanking the Lord Lieutenant for venturing over into Essex to do the job. I am glad he got this richly earned award just before he died.

By the 1970s the garden was beginning to develop and I should like to speak of two more people who have influenced me greatly and have been generous donors to the garden. One is Notcutt's fabled propagator Ivan Dickings (of whom Beth Chatto has said 'Ivan could put roots on bootlaces') and the other Maurice Mason, from whom I got most of the hardwood trees in the Top Garden.

As a Trustee of the Fullers Mill Trust, which we established for a while to sustain the garden, Ivan Dickings has been a great ally. He has given me more trees and shrubs and plants than I can possibly remember. He has an impressive ability to name rare plants and always comes laden. It is good still to enjoy Ivan's company as a friend. Maurice was also a generous provider, a great plantsman and holder of the RHS's Victoria Medal of Honour, who lived at Fincham and had another, larger garden at Larchwood, which included a Pinetum, where in total there were over two hundred acres. One drove slowly in the car around the garden and if you happened to comment favourably on a tree or shrub you were apt to find a potted specimen in the boot of your car after lunch, that is if you were sober enough to find anything. No matter what you said you liked to drink, you were given a small silver goblet full of it. How I ever got back from those liquid lunches I do not remember, but the boot was always full of plants.

One day visiting some of the glasshouses I noticed a potful of a small iris in full bloom and I asked Maurice where he got it from. He sent for his secretary who looked it up in the Accession Book and said the plant came from Mr Bernard Tickner, naming the date. Both of us had forgotten the occasion. I said I had lost my plant so Maurice at once gave me half of it. It was all tremendous good fun and illustrative of the plantsman's dictum 'if you want to keep a plant, give it away'.

I have particularly happy memories of being taken regularly by Maurice to the annual dinner of the Garden Society, effectively an exclusive dining club for titled and distinguished amateur gardeners. Only one professional was ever invited, Harold Hillier of the Winchester Nurseries and Arboretum. I would meet Maurice for a drink in the Savoy, where he was staying, and we would make our way to wherever the dinner was to take place. After an invariably splendid meal, those members and guests who had brought a plant or piece of plant material would talk about it. Harold Hillier usually rounded things off. I suppose these were evenings that contributed to my horticultural education almost as much as they did to my social standing as a gardener!

But we get older. Once, when Maurice was being taken on his daily tour of the garden, going very slowly because of his ill-heath, his car caught fire because it had been going so slowly for so long. The nurse who was driving managed to get him out of the car before he was engulfed; he was a heavy man but fortunately she was very strong.

Alas, the gardens did not survive long after Maurice's death in 1993. Although I imagine the trees have, I don't want to go back. I prefer to remember it as in the old days. One of Maurice's last acts was to propose me as a member of the International Dendrology Society and I remember paying the vast sum of £75 for a life membership which I still enjoy today.

## Plant hunting with Bess

Bess was enthusiastic about the wild flowers of Norway, as I was about ours, and this gave us a common link, although it meant I had to learn the Norwegian names, the Latin names and the English names of a lot of species new to me. Bess's knowledge of fungi became another common interest. And so we studied and took pleasure in plants together. We began to explore the mountains of Europe which, of course, included Norway. We went to the Alps, where in my twenties I had first skied with my cousins, staying as a paying guest with the villagers at Feldis in the Grisons, and striving to make our thirty pounds holiday allowance last a fortnight by cashing in international postage stamps at the local post-office. Now with Bess I returned to places I knew from later skiing expeditions to the Bernese Oberland further west, to hidden valleys and rushing waterfalls below the Jungfrau and the Eiger. Where I had skied, we now sought out spectacular flora. I remember still a magnificent example of the Lady's Slipper orchid, Cypripedium calceolus, which had been pointed out to me by the local parson, in full bloom in the snow.

We also visited the central Pyrenees on the Spanish side, the enchanted mountains of the Encantadas in Ariège. They really do have some kind of special appeal in springtime with the calls of capercaillie echoing around in the forest. At lower levels in the valleys there are large meadows full of Narcissus poeticus, the poet's daffodil, sweetly scented and a magnificent sight in May and therefore in the garden here the latest to flower. It was high above this in a small ravine one year that I discovered a lot of fritillaries in bloom. From this group we selected the most yellow of the different forms which is now named after me called Fritillaria pyrenaica 'Bernard Tickner'.

When we went to the Dolomites we took with us Reginald Farrer's classic work *King Laurin's Garden* published in 1913. He wrote in such great detail that it was possible to walk on one of the mountain paths following his description: 'on your right hand side if you look behind a big boulder there is a colony of a prostrate plant on the north side'. And so we went on, using the book as a companion to finding plants which he had described many years before.

We then went to Turkey and the Atlas mountains, which we visited many times, and this led us to Greece. Here we went to all the classical sights, impressive in themselves and rich in flora, and I have vivid memories of Olympia which we saw on our own, noone else around and nightingales singing in the bushes. We climbed Mount Olympus right up to the top, using hand and foot holes to be able to do it, and stayed in the refuge overnight. It was Greece which held our imagination. While we were there I learnt the Greek alphabet to be able to read; although I may not have understood the words, I could at least look them up and gradually I got a smattering of the language. From the main land we then started to visit the islands: Rhodes with its own flora and Symi and then Cyprus, which we visited a number of times, both the Greek side and the Turkish. We even had an apartment in what used to be called Nicosia.

This all led us to Crete with its magnificent flora and we travelled there many times across what I would think would be a span of thirty years. We loved walking the Gorge of Samaria in the days before it was shut until mid summer. Early in the year we had to wade through water criss-crossing our path as we went down the Gorge, seeing how the spring developed from the high mountains above with crocuses and early spring flowers, then as you came down early summer with peonies in bloom and asphodels and finally mid summer right at the bottom. Once I remember we stayed in a little cottage at the bottom of the Gorge with a wash basin and water jug and a donkey in the meadow outside. Then, walking back up again to where the car was we met by chance an Englishwoman, Chloe Darling, who was to become a good friend and back home would introduce us to Therfield Heath, the reserve near Royston with its colonies of rare pasque flowers. We finished the expedition staying that night in the refuge at the top, now quite a popular restaurant. On another occasion we walked up the mountains behind the Gorge in beautiful sunny weather and finally to the top, from where you could see north and south of the island and the sea on both sides. Idyllic times.

We used to tour the island and stay in the mountain villages and ask where a particular plant could be found and the normal reaction amongst the Cretans was that is was no good digging that plant up as it was not good to eat. This, in their view, was the only possible reason for doing so. I remember once being stopped by a man on a motorbike who came to see what I was doing, digging in the turf. I was in the middle of a long operation, digging around a root of Mandrake, Mandragora officinarum. I told him I was trying to dig this up to cook for my supper. I think he went away convinced of the madness of the English. Eventually I did manage to dig up the large tuberous rooted plant, a great testimony to Bess's patience as she waited for me, and subsequently it was planted in the garden. However, it did not thrive. I only discovered the reason years later when I found that our gardener at that time, Cecil Heyhoe, had been trying to get rid of it.

Bess by this time had become an expert plant finder and she would be ranging whilst I was either photographing or digging up plants to bring back. One notable plant that Bess found was an iris which used to be called Iris cretensis which was white instead of its normal colours of violet and lavender. We dug some up and left the majority and when we returned home I sent some to Kew and spoke with the Iris man there. He said at once that it had never been named before and asked who found it. When I said it was Bess he suggested I name it after her so I did and I have now distributed Iris cretensis 'Bess Tickner' amongst my friends, on the aforementioned principle of wanting to retain a plant by giving it away.

I should say that prior to one of these trips to Greece or Crete I would often make sure I visited my friend John Raven at Docwra Manor in Shepreth. Now perhaps to be identified as the father of the media gardener Sarah Raven, John was a classics don and distinguished botanist, the author of the 1971 work *A Botanist's Garden.* He had an amazing memory for the locations of plants and if you could get him to do it he would recall individual plants from his travels and where they were.

I remember once he told me of a yellow form of Ranunculus asiaticus growing on an acropolis in eastern Crete. He said if I dug at such and such a point in the bare ground I would find its dormant tubers. We went to the site, but were obliged to wait our turn because the guardian was showing round some German archaeologists. They wanted to know every detail and their guide went on and on and on and we had to wait hours before we dared approach the site to dig. We got our hidden treasure at last, however, and grew it in the garden over several years. It is a beautiful yellow flower with a black boss in the middle of it. John was a very friendly man and his wife, Faith, was welcoming too. I used to make a detour on my trips to Biggleswade to visit the Greene King Brewery there to see John and it was always a pleasure. When he died the church at Shepreth was full of plants from the garden, which Faith had collected.

A fair proportion of the plants we collected have gone now from the garden after thriving for a number of years but there are still many from Crete still growing here, those I have described on the terraces, for example, and others like the Spiny Spurge Euphorbia acanthothamnos, the Valonia Oak on the Patch and Arum ideaum from the slopes of Mount Ida, the highest mountain on the island. It is a rare plant in cultivation which I have found on the way up to the top of the gorge of Samaria growing in quantity under subshrubs in the shade.

## One other Collector's Story

Not all my acquisitions have been from the mountains and islands of Europe, of course, and one striking plant hails from much nearer home. I was reminded of the story by meeting in the garden recently a lady who had lived with her family at Cavenham Mill, the former home of the artist Alfred Blundell and his wife Eva. They were great friends of mine whom I used to visit quite frequently, sometimes in the winter walking down the river path, impassable in summer, to Lackford Bridge and then over the fields to Cavenham. It took up to two hours, depending on the density of the weeds. Alfred was always a good source of amusing stories. He died in 1968 while Eva carried on for a few more years before her arthritis meant she had to leave the Mill.

Every year Alfred used to have a big vase of colchicums in his studio; they were the white ones, Colchicum sp. 'Album' which were growing in his woodland. Once the Blundells had left Cavenham Mill, however, there was talk of redevelopment so, remembering the colchicums in his studio, I went with Bess in Autumn to see if I could find them in his woodland. It must have been early in the 1970s. I found them and dug some up to take home. When I looked them up in a catalogue I found to my astonishment they were £6 a tuber. I was so astonished in fact that greed overcame me and I went back to dig up some more. For my pains I got stung by a very angry bee, no doubt annoyed by my greed, and I came home abashed!

So I was pleased to be able to give some colchicum tubers to the lady who had lived at Cavenham subsequent to Alfred's demise when the Mill was still in its 'wild state'. This was her description and I understood perfectly what she meant. Like her I preferred the original state before it was 'improved'.

Before he died Alfred gave us a wedding present of one of his watercolours, which I still enjoy to this day. It hangs in a prime position in the house because it so typifies the area. It is of a winter scene of the view from his studio window and shows the Mill Pool with the heathlands behind and the woodland on the left, a truly wild scene.

Today, we have many Colchicum speciosum 'Album' plants,

hundreds I would say, and they all derive from that single digging. Greed or no greed!

## The Principles of Collecting

With my childhood love of collecting butterflies, moths and plants it can come as no surprise to the reader that I was a great digger up of plants in the wild, making raids on wild plants in Greece and, in particular, in Crete where Bess and I searched the mountains for thirty years. We brought back many interesting species. However, it is important to say that none were listed as forbidden under the Convention on International Trade in Endangered Species of Wild Fauna and Flora (CITES), plants such as cyclamen. Originally we used to get a plant import licence which meant that on arrival in the UK we had to hand a list of the plants we had collected to the Customs. An officer then worked ponderously through the list of prohibited plants, like potatoes and beet species, not knowing scientific names or really what we were talking about but determined to do his duty. After that I sent a list of our plants in to the then Ministry of Agriculture and undertook that they could be inspected at any time and if necessary destroyed but noone ever came. So I have no concerns when accused of taking plants from the wild.

I know that many people have strong views on digging up any wild plants but there is a great difference between the wholesale digging up of rarities – collecting large quantities of a single species, for example crocuses or cyclamen, for sale on the open market – and taking from a colony of thousands the occasional single plant whose absence could not possibly be detected – collecting responsibly, as I would always hope to do. I know the argument that it is all very well provided everyone doesn't do the same thing, but of course they don't, and never have done. I believe it is quite ridiculous to shout in horror when limited digging in a large colony occurs or sample pieces from a newly discovered variety are taken, provided that the great majority of plant material is left in the wild.

## Plants for the Garden

Up to now I have referred to many of the plants in Fullers Mill Garden and talked about the way in which many have come here, without making many general statements about my choices. So here goes. Firstly, I prefer plants which are species (the original wild plant form) rather than hybrids. This isn't a rule which is never to be broken, particularly in the case of lilies, because there are some excellent modern hybrids of plants but of these I prefer the ones that look like the species. In my view they retain the delicacy and clarity that so often is lost in over-hybridising.

Plants for the garden also have to have good foliage. This is particularly necessary because of my red/green colour blindness, inherited from my maternal grandfather. This makes it very difficult to distinguish between pink and blue, and purple and mauve defeat me. The only colours I feel confident about are yellow, which is a very striking colour for me, and white. There is perhaps a preponderance of these in the garden as a consequence but I am not good at doing any kind of design with colour in a border. I am quite happy to receive praise for what I have achieved but it is ill-deserved. Any effectiveness is quite fortuitous.

So, as I learnt from Christopher Lloyd, foliage is the most important feature of a plant, lasting so much longer than its flowers. The fineness of grasses, the corrugation of Veratrum nigrum and the leaves of Hosta plantaginea grandiflora, the tropical look of Melianthus Major – interesting foliage is of the greatest importance to me when planting as I try to build a sympathetic although contrasting structural design from the height, architecture and foliage and colour, if I can imagine it, of neighbouring plants.

Focusing on specific plants, there are three collections made over the years which run through the garden, those of Euphorbias, Peonies and species Lilies.

## Euphorbias

I can't really remember how euphorbias were introduced into the garden because I can remember the days when I actually disliked them; with their bold foliage they are distinctly different from the majority of herbaceous plants. However, I must have had some euphorbias in the garden when my interest was certainly accelerated by a chance seedling from Euphorbia x martini, which was itself a chance hybrid in nature. I thought E x martini was sterile and it was this that first made me look closely at this seedling which had probably arisen from a nearby plant of the hybrid Euphorbia characias subsp. wulfenii 'Purple and Gold.' The new form was a handsome and distinctive plant. I thought it of some value and exhibited it for an award from the RHS which in 1999 gave it an Order of Merit. I then went to Notcutts Nursery and suggested they might like to trial the plant with a view to my giving them sole propagating rights. They agreed and did trials and decided to launch the new seedling under the name 'Redwing'. This was because in winter the 'nose' of the plant became red and the bracts were a darker green, the colder the weather. Eventually the nose lifted and became in effect the flower of the plant which covered the plant itself with bright yellow inflorescence so you could barely see a leaf. This was the attraction of the plant which required hardly any marketing behind it. It was said to walk out of Garden Centres, being in bloom on Mothers' Day in March and lasting for several months into the summer. It sold like hot cakes. 'Redwing' got a further award from the RHS in 2000, a First Class certificate, and in 2002 was awarded a further Order of Merit. We were getting royalties from Notcutts of between six and eight thousand pounds per year and then in 2010, after Woods had taken over the Nursery side of Notcutts, we got over £10,000 in the year. It depends on where the plant is being marketed: when you go to a different part of the world it generates a surge of sales which is reflected in the royalties.

After several years of this Notcutts told me a new variety had emerged which was completely different from 'Redwing' and asked if I should like to see it. I went to the trial grounds and saw this maroon-purple foliaged euphorbia of the same habit as Redwing but completely different in its colour. I asked how it had happened and was told it was just a chance variety occurring during propagation and so it would not be covered under our agreement. My response was that I had an agreement with them over the sole propagating rights of the material I had given to them but had placed no restrictions on the varieties to which it should apply. I asked them where they had got the source material for this new plant and they had to say from me! To avoid a clashing of swords with solicitors we agreed to split the difference and I accepted a lower rate of royalty for this new variety which was to be called 'Blackbird'. I suppose that 'Blackbird' gets its colouring from the genetic material of x 'Purple and Gold' but no one can be sure about this. There seem to be more than one clone about because Ivan Dickings regards it as an unstable type of plant whereas for other gardeners it is secure and a fine addition to the garden. There was a planting of 'Blackbird' here in autumn 2010 and in that case it did not prove reliable.

My experiences with our introductions naturally increased my interest in the genus as a whole and many other plants came as a result, including Euphorbia griffithii, E.x.pasteurii and the most dramatic of them all Euphorbia stygiana from the Azores, which turned out to be quite hardy and hardier than its neighbour Euphorbia mellifera from Madeira which we also have in the garden.

## Peonies

I am always interested in peonies because of their delicacy of flower. They are so fleeting and you are lucky in some cases if

the flowers last a week but they are always simple and in clear colours so that I try to grow as many of the species as I can. We have a good number of herbaceous forms in the garden, among them Paeonia clusii and mascula on the terraces and elsewhere the Caucasians mlokosewitschii (Molly-the-Witch) and tenuifolia, the Balkan peregrina, P. emodi the Himalayan peony and veitchii from China.

We also have tree peonies from China, including the rare paeonia rockii, white with a maroon centre. This is from Ivan Dickings who created a plant for me from his own, itself derived from Sir Frederick Stern's original. My first plant came to grief when one of the gardeners cut off all the potential flowering buds for the season because they looked untidy, which they did – but he should have asked me first. This killed the plant. Ivan's replacement was in turn a flourishing clump in the border opposite the Bothy until the bucket of digger used to form a trench for the water supply swung around and knocked off all the grafts of this new plant, perhaps the rarest in the whole garden. We rushed the components back to Ivan who arranged for them to be re-grafted. I hope three times will be lucky but to be sure we have had alternative supplies from Dr Doug Joyce, two seedlings each from two different sources. In the event just one of the sources has given good white flowers like rockii, though to be sure I am glad to have all the resulting plants in the garden.

Finally, shrub peonies. My particular favourites must include Paeonia delavayi which is very dark maroon with a small simple flower, and then there is a yellow one, P. ludlowii lutea whose leaves quite often grow so quickly that they almost cover the blooms hidden in the foliage.

## Lilies

I first got interested in lilies because in the early days I was looking for some plants which would really lift the scene. The garden had an immature aspect at that time and lilies filled the gap. I followed up my interest through the original Lily and Iris Group that once functioned under Jenny Robinson and the Benton Enders at Hadleigh and this led me to join the Lily Group of the RHS. I much enjoyed their functions over the years, and got to know Derek Fox who wrote a very influential book on lily species and created some hybrid lilies using species from the West Coast of America. I used to go to see Derek in his garden and choose lilies from there and from his allotment. Most of them, I fear, I have now lost, but I do still have one plant which has survived twenty-five years in the garden. It is an easy going but beautiful hybrid called 'Lake Tulare', a demure and small flowered lily with long pedicels which displays the flowers in a delicate way. It is this delicacy that I enjoy and prefer to the gross appearance of many other hybrids. I have kept 'Lake Tulare' going by the simple expedient of every few years lifting the clump in the autumn, spitting it up and replanting in good fertile, well drained soil.

Inspired by Derek I set about collecting species lilies which would grow in our soil. We still have a great number such as Lilium pardalinum and the turkscap Bellingham hybrids, L.monadelphum, lilium leichtlinii from Japan, the Chinese tiger lily Lilium henryi and Lilium pyrenaicum, from the Pyrenees but now, I understand, naturalised and growing wild in this country. They all do well for us, alongside many of the better hybrids such as highly scented Trumpet lilies and the new race, trumpets crossed with oriental lilies, which are lime tolerant and are far more attractive than their ugly name Orienpets might lead you to expect.

The Garden holds many more treasures that the three collections I have described here. Some are specimens unique to the garden, like the elegant birch trees we call 'Silver Grace', growing in a semi-circle by the entrance gate, or the variegated Honesty, Lunaria rediviva 'Honour Bright', down by the pond. Others are of interest in themselves: Cardiocrinum giganteum, monocarpic with chartreuse lily flowers, and galanthus galore. They come from around the world and we can have a snowdrop in flower in the garden from October to May. In 2011 Galanthus reginae-olgae, a variety from Greece, came into bloom at the end of August ... I feel, however, that I should leave some plants for readers to find for themselves if this chapter has whetted the appetite and they decide to visit Fullers Mill for themselves. I'll close this chapter instead with some thoughts on

## Mushrooms

Bess and I used to eat quite a wide variety of mushrooms growing wild in this part of Suffolk. It was Bess who first introduced me to this because in her native Norway such foraging was commonplace. Most Englishmen in my day, coming across some fungi on a walk in the countryside, would look at them and give them a good kicking, and would feel a better citizen for having done so, striding on with a dim sense of having benefited humanity. Yet on the edge of walks in big cities like Bergen and Oslo there would be identification facilities so when you brought your crop back from a walk you could have it checked for any that were poisonous. In actual fact there are very few poisonous mushrooms. There are a large number that can give you temporary illness or have no merit in their flavour and then there are quite a large number of edible ones, some of which I will describe. All of this was well known to Bess and if she could say 'I know this mushroom and it tastes of this, that or the other.' I would be content. But if she said 'I am not quite sure. We will look it up when we get back', I would say 'No, thank you.' It's not worth the risk. The fungus that could make you seriously ill or even kill you is Amanita phalloides, the deathcap mushroom, to be avoided at all cost. The white form resembles many edible species but its stem has a vulva which easily and quickly identifies it.

To start the season we used to get parasol mushrooms growing out in the open on light soil. They had a special flavour, difficult to describe (some say they have the odour and taste of maple syrup) but very characteristic. I suppose it was the ordinary field mushrooms which came in next – they take a lot of beating for flavour. They are easily identified but one has to be aware of the similar Yellow Staining mushroom which when cut exudes yellow 'sap'. This can make you vomit and gives you diarrhoea. So is to be avoided.

Then in the woods there were wood mushrooms, smaller with dark heads and growing in profusion in some years. One year, when the temperature and the rainfall were right, there were such quantities of them, we picked so many that we made mushroom extract from them. We reduced it down, cooled it and poured it into ice cube trays. We ended with plastic bags full of cubes of the most delicious extract which you could use in casseroles or put into mushroom soup to transform it with a high octane mushroom taste. Chanterelles are a great early mushroom. Here, alas, we only had 'false' chanterelles which are not good at all but in Bergen the real thing was plentiful and delicious when cooked. In West Stow Country Park there were open slopes where Ink Caps used to proliferate and we used to collect from there. They were quite good to eat but you quickly had enough of them and you were keen to move onto something else.

Later on in the season the various Boletus species started to appear and there was one particular variety Bess enjoyed eating which used to grow deep in the grass verge. It was quite short and needed a keen eye to find it, but find it Bess did. I found it rather slimy to eat and didn't care for it. Then when our friend Richard left the Country Park we came into a windfall because he showed us his chief spots for collecting ceps or porcini or Boletus edulis – all the same thing. It would often be the end of October before these appeared but they were worth collecting as they had one of the most delicious flavours. I do remember one year we had a good haul of different types of mushrooms from walking around the Country Park and it was only when we got home that someone told us that a group on an organised Fungus Foray had been behind us. They found themselves following a trail of cut and collected mushrooms and all they got were the remains. I didn't dare tell them we were the ones who had been collecting in front of them. I think the last mushrooms which we ate were Blewits which sometimes appeared on the grass verges alongside the track coming down to the house but there was another good spot for them on the heath, by the beginning of the Icknield Way. The fruiting very much depended on the rainfall and the weather at this time of the year, which was of course rather variable, and the frost would stop it all.

Occasionally some of these mushrooms I have described would appear mysteriously in the garden but they always appeared to be more sinister than those we found further afield. I can't remember that we ever ate any from the garden.

# Chapter Eleven

# The Wildlife of Fullers Mill

### Changes in bird life

A few years before I came here, when I was living at The Chantry in Bury St Edmunds, a farmer told me he had seen in a field of rye on the edge of the Elveden Estate a group of six or seven Great Bustards. I could hardly believe this but I went out to see and there they were. In those days I had no connection with any organisation to whom I could report so that it has never been corroborated but they could hardly have been any other kind of bird given the surroundings and the height of the rye which must have been all of five feet.

Since then there have been many changes in local bird life due to the changes of habitat here as well as national trends. Originally, before the gravel company came, Bess and I enjoyed simple walks through the meadows where Ken Curtis's cows were grazing with ample cow pats, the insect life which flowed from them and, as a consequence, plenty of swallows, house martins and swifts, though no sand martins. We used to walk often in a summer evening and my memories of spring time include the drumming of snipe, lapwing in aerial display and the call of redshank everywhere. The latter were very common and I remember being able to imitate their call and bring them right to the house; I can still see one bird sitting on the garden seat after I had called it over. These are all species largely missing now the gravel lakes have replaced the pastures, though we do get an occasional lapwing nesting on the meadows and coming down to the Reserve.

Not everything has been lost from those days. In an earlier chapter I recalled how on those evening walks Bess and I heard nightingales and were buzzed by nightjars. Well, I know that on the Reserve nowadays there are generally four or five singing nightingales, males with their females and nests. It may be that like us they like to have neighbours, not too close to invade their personal territory but within earshot. Near to the Visitor Centre there is an area of hawthorn, sloe and similarly-sized shrubs with grassy patches in between which is good habitat in which the nightingales can nest and feed. It is an area also enjoyed by the tree sparrows which have become almost as rare nationally as the nightingales.

The nightjars, too, have returned. The Corsican Pine trees beside the track had only just been planted when I arrived here in 1958. The majority of the land was open within a perimeter of mature trees, with just an occasional tree on the heath. It provided a first class habitat for nightjars. By the 1990s, however, the trees had grown and we heard them no more. Then, several years ago, this part of the forest was thinned and five or six acres clear felled north of the house towards the road. Two years later it was planted with Scots Pine seedlings. I had never known this species used before. It was done because nearly all the Corsican Pine in the forest is diseased with Red Band Needle Blight so it can no longer be planted. The Scots Pine will take double the amount of time to mature, though. The wood is open once again and once again I can hear the nightjar 'churring'.

Last night I went outside and saw the moon rise in the south. I thought it would come over the house but instead it was at a low angle and set in the horizon to the East so that around nine o'clock it was still moderately light. Listening, I hear the noise of the river and still many birds calling. Now I walk away from the water to improve the possibility of hearing the nightjar. I use the old army practice of listening for noises in the quiet by turning my back to the sounds I want to hear and cupping my ears to catch the faintest noises more clearly. Blackbirds are singing and robins everywhere. I hear a cuckoo in the distance. A wood pigeon seems to perform a set sequence, followed by one more distant and, still further off, one or two beyond. On the Reserve there is a noisy chorus from the blackheaded gull colony and an occasional outburst from the greylag geese settling down for the night. Gradually they fade into silence. It has got slightly darker but there are still robins and blackbirds calling at half past nine in the dusk. A heron flies over on its way to the heronry in the forest with a single, distinctively raucous call; the occasional moorhen and carrion crow can be heard and slowly the noise ceases. It is strange but after the last blackbird the cuckoo still continues and it and the robin are the last birds calling as the light fades. Then, as dusk becomes night, it is almost 10 pm, I hear the long 'churring' of the nightjar. It is an extraordinary noise – mechanical but not in a metallic sense. To me, it sounds as though the pitch changes but the bird book says this is what you hear when the nightjar turns its head.

Being a ground nesting bird the nightjar camouflages its nest extremely well but it is still prone to be predated by hedgehogs, which eat both its eggs and its young. Hedgehogs also predate woodlarks. Nightjars and woodlarks are the main reason why the whole of the King's Forest has been designated a Site of Special Scientific Interest (SSSI). For me, however, the Special Interest of our site lies elsewhere. It is in the abrupt change of habitat which exists between the lakes and the forest, with the River Lark running between the two. Geese and water birds to the south and to the north woodland and heathland and, once more, ideal country for nightjars.

With the first lake formed Bess and I used to walk around it in the evening with our golden Labrador and the two cats who came as well. There would be woodcock roaming backwards and forwards from the wood, over the lake to the forest and long eared bats hawking insects over the lake. These have all gone now although the habitat is perfect so there must be some other cause that I don't know of. We had a colony of bats in the house as a summer roost, between the ceiling of the attic and the roof space. They were mostly Pipistrelles and once a year Bess and I counted them as they emerged in the summer evenings. This annual count was a ritual which was quite hard to perform as the bats emerged at the same time both from the roof and from holes under the barge boards. I remember one year the girl who was organising the counting for Suffolk Wildlife Trust was very keen and wanted us to count them on several occasions. We said we would just do it the once so she settled for that and gave us a date. I remember she was Irish and she added a PS: 'if it's wet, count them the day before!' For the last few summers we have not had any bats in the house so I suppose they have found an alternative place to roost.

Gradually as more lakes appeared, more or less from Lackford Bridge right along here to Flempton Bridge, the bird count rapidly followed the change in habitat. Notable sightings over the years have included Golden Eye on the deep water lakes in the Lackford meadows in the wintertime and Goosanders in the river and in the shallower lakes near the SWT Visitor Centre. We have Bitterns over-wintering here now: they like the rushes on the shallow edges of the lakes which make them extremely difficult to see but we cannot retain them for breeding because we do not have large enough reed beds. I expect they go to the big marshy areas on the East Coast to breed. In the summertime we have stone curlew back breeding on the meadows of the Reserve which is a great achievement and we get an occasional Osprey fishing in the shallower waters. It would be good habitat for their breeding and I hope one day this may come about. Barn Owls now nest in the locality. It was discovered that there were not enough holes for barn owls in West Suffolk where barns have been repaired, turned into holiday lets or demolished, unlike in East Suffolk where there are still some crumbling buildings. So a campaign was started by SWT to put up barn owl boxes, to inspect them regularly and to ring any fledglings. We have been proud to take part in this at Fullers Mill with a first successful breeding in 2011. The habitat is good and I believe there are plenty of short-tailed field voles, owls' chief prey, but the population of these does vary from year to year, the breeding success of barn owls fluctuating accordingly.

There is much more to be said about changes to bird life due to alteration in habitat and I have included an alphabetical list commenting on species in an appendix.

## Talking with Swans

We have had Swans here for over fifty years. There have always been swans on the River Lark or the Culford Stream or the Mill Deep lake and we have been on increasingly close terms. At first sight a swan is not the kind of creature that you might feel it is feasible to get close to but they respond to talking and in spite of the name Mute Swan are not without speech in response. They have nested either in the garden or around the lake and it has been our good fortune to be involved in this process. When a decision has been made by the pair to choose a site and to start to collect material we have generally helped.

Bess in particular took a great interest in this and cut and provided suitable material to build into the nest. It was always the pen, the female, who selected the site, and it was ever thus.

If you have ever watched a family on the beach deciding where to have a picnic, it is always the female of the species who makes the decision. It is no good the father plonking things down somewhere because the mother will say it is too windy and move on; only when she has reached a satisfactory site can the male put down the heavy gear. And so it is with swans.

Most of the books say that the incubation is shared by the pair and although this is true the vast majority of it is carried out by the pen and the cob only takes over occasionally in the later stages. The majority of the time the incubation is taking place the cob is protecting the feeding territory very aggressively and his targets have included me and Bess as well as our cats, who normally came with us when we were feeding the birds but were quickly scared away by the great hissing and opening of wings which took place if they got close. Bess was also frightened of the cob and he knew this and would chase her vigorously but I would have none of it and would advance on him with my arms fully extended, parallel to the ground, to simulate wings and he would always retreat with a certain amount of hissing. I think swans, like every good shop steward, know to within an inch how far they can take you, and react accordingly. In our situation on the lake the cob spent most of his time chasing geese and never quite catching one, because as he got closer the goose would fly on a few paces and the process would start all over again. But occasionally a young non-breeding swan, one or two years old, would stray onto the lake. The cob would immediately attack it and, if it had not got the sense to get onto the bank or fly off, it could be killed. The youngster would be driven into one of the corners of the lake. Then the cob would catch it by the back of the neck and drown it, standing on it with his big feet until it was dead. This extreme aggression is, I think, intuitively designed to conserve the food for the family and the aggression continues until the young are well grown. Occasionally a cob will kill a goose if he can catch one but he will always tolerate smaller fry: ducks, coots and moorhens escape unmolested and unharmed unless they interfere with the actual feeding process. There are plenty of stories of people being attacked by swans and having their arms broken but, although the front of the wing of the cob is very hard, I have been struck by it on a number of occasions and survived. A swan battle is a frightening experience and always gives rise to public concern, with telephone calls to the SWT office – 'Come at once. One swan is killing another one.' These concerns require a tactful response but should never lead to intervention.

Towards the end of incubation, I am always drawn to the nest by the unusual presence of the cob, who is invariably present at the hatching. I suppose the young cygnets are now making a noise inside the eggs which draws him to show interest. By this time the pen has been sitting on the nest for about thirty-five days, only coming off occasionally to wash and feed so she is particularly run down.

The nest is always close to the waterside and sometimes over the years pens have chosen sites which unfortunately get flooded. I remember one year in particular when the nest was surrounded by flood water which backed up the stream from the river so with a scythe I got rushes and passed them to Bess who placed them on either side of the nest. She and the pen built up the height of the nest so that it was two or three inches higher and safe from the rising waters. This was a wonderful collaborative achievement. When the waters subsided the nest looked an absurdly high edifice with considerable problems of access, but it saved the day.

On hatching the cygnets remain in the nest for about two days before they are led out onto the water where pen and cob feed them with tiny morsels of swan food. This is a selection of submerged aquatics which I have not identified but is very particular to the swans. It is a wonderful sight to see cygnets with their families and particularly when they tired and they clamber aboard one of the parents, generally the pen who then has to adjust her alignment according to the spread of weight. There is a delightful downy area under the swan's wings into which the cygnets can nestle and snooze. In hot weather, before the cygnets have left the nest, the swan will shade the cygnets from the sun whilst enduring the heat herself.

Bess and I have enjoyed feeding the swans with wheat and this is where we trained our swans to talk to us. I used to give a questioning snort as I approached and after a time the swan would repeat the sound back to me, eventually taking the initiative and snorting a greeting as I approached. Facially it is extremely difficult to tell one swan from another but by this means we have been able to keep in touch with individual birds over many years.

We had one old cob who had lost his mate and must have been twenty years old at least. He was being roughed up by younger ones who wanted him out of their territory. If he went into the river he got attacked, so we had to provide for him on the side with a washing-up bowl of water to drink from. At his age he was getting very arthritic and walking was a difficulty. Eventually we got in touch with the Swan Rescue Service who came to collect him. They bandaged him up so that he was immobilized for the car journey and the last we saw of him was looking through the back window of the car. Later that day the Rescue Service telephoned to say they had put him into an enclosure with an elderly pen. They were very pleased to have him because it was so unusual to get a swan with nothing physically wrong with him other than old age. Unfortunately most of their clients were sick, with fish hooks or lead shot in them.

One year we had a pair of swans that nested near the stream and towards the end of the incubation the pen seemed to be in some distress. It was only when I got up close that I realised she was losing her sight and after a few days she had long periods off the nest and then a day or two later she disappeared. The cob took over and stuck it for a day or two. Then one morning as I was walking by I saw she had returned and I witnessed a sight I had never heard of, nor have I seen before or since. It really was quite dramatic. There was a great intertwining of necks and gentle recognition signals, audible and visual, which went on for several minutes until the pen took over the incubation again. It was a very moving experience for me. I have seen something similar with great crested grebes but in their case it has always been on the water. I am wondering whether it was a moving experience for the swans. Do they have emotions or is it simply a natural reaction of recognition and bonding? By this stage we knew the pen was completely blind because she didn't react to a hand waved in front of her face. Because of this, I suppose, she was unable to feed and eventually deserted the nest and never came back. The cob continued to incubate for a few more days and then gave up and I expect the eggs had been left too long and had got cold between the comings and goings and so never hatched. This was a sad end to a story.

In 2012 we had a different kind of drama. Our last family had ten successive broods here, nesting mostly round the lake in different places, but the last nest ended in disaster. Annie, our Head Gardener, came into the house to say a swan was dead and floating on the lake and I went to look and discovered it was the pen who was dead and the nest and eggs destroyed. I cannot think of any animal that would have done this other than a human one and I am afraid it was a case of vandalism which was very distressing to me and I suppose a great loss to the cob. He hung around and was fed for a few days but then disappeared. However, the good news to finish with is that the cob then found another mate. They must have re-nested, possibly on the far side of the island which was obscured from view by the weeping willow, for although I had seen the cob coming up to feed regularly I had assumed wrongly that he was solitary. Then in late July the pen appeared with three very small newly hatched cygnets. This was a great joy. We had never had small cygnets so late in the year. I only hope they were large enough to get through the winter.

Every morning when I walk along beside the river with a bucket of grain I see the current family of swans – two adults and five cygnets – and in December as I write this they are now pretty well full grown and beginning to show flecks of white in their grey plumage. There seems to be a tradition amongst swans that the pen always leads and the cob brings up the rear and as I walk alongside them to find a suitable place to start to throw the grain into the river a chorus comes up from the cygnets which I describe as wittering. That word seems to fit the nice little noise they all make whilst I snort recognition signals with the cob. It is following every morning the same routine as to where I throw the grain and how I do it that unites us. The other thing I have noticed, which is rather endearing and reminiscent of something engrained in families, whatever species, the world over, is that the adults always hold back to allow the cygnets to come forward to have the first food. They only start eating when they are satisfied that there is sufficient thrown out for all to enjoy.

Every three or four weeks the whole family chooses a remote area in which to feed, no doubt on the roots of aquatic plants because in midwinter there is nothing else; I suppose the grain I give them does not supply everything they need from food. Swans will, if circumstances develop, graze on grass, like geese, but they need to be pretty hungry to do that. Eventually, a stage is reached in the development of the cygnets at which the adults inevitably turn on them and do not allow them access to the water to the consternation of the youngsters. They stand about disconcerted on the banks and any attempt to return to the water gets rebuffed rigorously. What is happening here is, of course, the protection of the environment and food supply for the following year. The parents continue this behaviour until the cygnets fly off which they do with difficulty because only by getting in the water can a swan get enough speed on the runway to take off. And even then it needs a good strong windy day to get a successful lift off to another area and to a new life.

## Barnyard Geese

There have been two stories about barnyard geese I might put in here and one starts when Nancy Curtis from the farm in the village got in touch with me to say a friend had asked her about a good home for some geese and she had told them about Fullers Mill. So I asked what they were – they were half breed Chinese Barnyard Geese – and  why they wanted to get rid of them. Nancy said  'You will have to ask the people concerned,' who were the Miss Keysers, two elderly ladies who lived at Burrough Green in the old Georgian rectory next to the church. I telephoned them and said that I was interested in their geese but wondered why they wanted to get rid of them They said they were on the move and didn't want to take these geese because they weren't very nice to the others. I was intrigued and said I would come over but they said no, they would let me know when I could take them.

'But you will be nice to them, won't you?'

Well, the weeks went by and then one day the Miss Keysers telephoned and said

'Come at once. We have the two geese in a loose box and cook is up a ladder waving a flag to stop them flying out.'

This was getting ever more strange so I grabbed an old box and some string and went over to Burrough Green expecting to see a fat cook and apron strings up a ladder. But it was Cook the stable boy up the ladder: in those days nobody had any Christian names. The sisters looked at me and my box and said again

'You will be nice to them, won't you?'

It wasn't going to be easy to get two geese into a small box and still be nice to them, however. I asked everyone to give me space and I managed it and brought them home but before I did so I asked what was happening. They told me they were moving all their wildlife, including their race horses and broken down horses, hens and ducks and geese, guinea fowl and peacocks to a new site, I think near Epsom. I asked how they were going to do it and Miss Keyser said they had been training all the animals for the great move by putting them into coops over night, 'Council houses, you know,' for the great lift off. I was then invited inside to find a large St Bernard dog occupying the whole of the sofa with a pug at its head. A voice behind me suddenly said ' Hello, dear'. I thought it was a Miss Keyser but it was a cockatoo which was part of the menagerie. I was taken outside and shown a whole lot of peacocks in a large Dutch barn that they had wired in the front to stop them flying out and as soon as we got within sight the birds started calling, letting off tremendous 'yahoos.' I asked what they were doing in there and Miss Keyser said they had been very naughty. People had complained that they flew around Newmarket and regularly descended on a newly dug and resurfaced grave in the churchyard next door, scratching energetically among the marble chippings used to finish it off. The family who had just buried a relative took exception to this behaviour, which led eventually to the peacocks being banned to the barn.

When I got home I put the geese into an enclosure I had made for them earlier. I clipped their primary wing feathers so they were not able to fly out of it and rang up the Miss Keysers that evening to say they had settled down well and were ok. But the next morning there was a very strong wind and somehow or another they did manage to fly out. I searched all round and eventually found them quietly grazing on one of greens at Flempton Golf Course, over a half a mile away as the goose flies.

I and a helper went over and got round the back of the geese and slowly walked them up; they ran and they ran and they ran and eventually took off into the wind and to our astonishment flew back to their enclosure. I was, after all, able to report to the Miss Keysers that they had settled in and all was well.

The next geese we had came from a friend who had hatched them and had brought them up on a tennis court at Norton. They were just ordinary white barnyard geese or Roman Geese as they are called. We thought it would be nice to have them at the Mill but when I released them by the river they didn't know what to do. They had never seen that extent of water before; the largest amount they had seen was in a washing-up bowl. We had to give them a washing-up bowl of water right beside the river until eventually they plucked up courage and swam in the Lark. It was also quite evident on the first night that they didn't know where to roost so I walked them up the river bank and left them under a willow tree where they seemed quite happy. Then every evening as it got dusk I had to repeat this performance until eventually they did it on their own.

One day after heavy rain there was a lot of water coming down the river and I saw the geese swimming in it. As I walked from upstream towards the house I saw a flight of ducks get up from the river and fly over my head and as I was watching them I became aware the geese had stopped swimming and were watching them too, motionless on the water, their heads moving from side to side to follow the flight. Then, in no time at all, because the river was flowing so strongly, the geese found themselves to their dismay swept over the sluice downstream and unceremoniously spilled out on the other side. I ran as fast as I could along the river bank as they floated fast downstream until, at the bend where the river was slower, I managed to stop and call them over to me. To my amazement and relief they came right over so that I could lift them out of the water and onto the bank. I carried them back up to their normal place beyond the sluice upstream and told them they really needed to keep paddling when they were on the river, though I think by that time they had realised that for themselves.

## Winter Wildlife

As the autumn gradually turns into Winter there follows a distinct change in the ways of the wildlife.

Firstly, the goslings begin to get into flocks as they become capable of flying. This induces a lot of local movement up and down the river and in the neighbouring lakes as competing flocks congregate and dissipate and reassemble. To some extent this applies to the swans on the river as their young fly off to try to find new feeding grounds or in some years join other families of cygnets in a winter feeding flock. Occasionally at this time we see wild swans, Bewicks coming in en route to Welney. They seem to use the Lark as a navigational highway and I expect it is quite useful even at night as it reflects the winter sky. Going out to mend a bonfire as darkness falls you hear in the distance a soft calling of Bewicks, which is a wonderful wild noise as they fly overhead on soundless wings – it is only Mute Swans that create noise with their wings.

Early in the autumn there is a large, increasing movement of gulls from all points of the compass to the lakes and especially the sailing lake. Again they seem to use the Lark, perhaps unconsciously, as a guideline to their destination. People say they even come to roost here overnight from the coast, which seems a big effort to get a night's sleep. It is a wonderful thing to watch their arrival. They are nearly all Black headed with some Common Gulls and a few Lesser Black-backs. They start arriving in mid afternoon in small parties of twenty and thirty and then as soon as one has flown over you see another one coming. It goes on like this hour after hour until darkness falls. Seen from below with a low sun which illuminates their white underparts they are a beautiful sight. And it is without sound. They come in silently, gliding effortlessly with barely a movement of their wings. I have never ever heard them give as much as a squawk, that is until they get to their destination on the sailing lake. Then they kick up the most infernal din to make up for their silent travel and continue to give voice all night. I stand outside the back door so that I can hear them and not be deafened by the flow of the river. They continue long after one would have liked to have been sleeping quietly.

Some years we get large flocks of starlings coming to roost in the reeds and this starts with parties, fifty to a hundred again, coming in quite low from all directions of the compass to the roost. There they find earlier parties assembling in an ever-increasing flock, swirling round the top of the lakes like a swarm of bees, a cloud, a phenomenon which has been remarked upon since Roman times. Now the whole flock moves as one and it is a fascinating sight to see until it gets so large that it almost fills the sky and then quite suddenly the whole lot goes down to roost with a distinct fluttering of wings and you are left feeling that you would like to applaud. It is truly one of the most dramatic sights in nature and the only problem is that it can't be relied upon to occur on a regular basis. This is because sparrowhawks regard the murmuration as an opportunity for 'fast food' and come in and take their toll. At first this is tolerated by the flock but eventually it gets split up and moves on.

As for the gulls, as winter progresses the number of gulls visiting the Reserve to roost grows to many thousands, I think up to 15,000 have been been recorded. Birdwatching gull specialists come and are able to say how many gulls are there.

Then they look at this vast flock before it dissipates and by some magic identify one Icelandic gull or one other named rarity, but unless you are standing close to the person making the identification the chances of seeing this one gull among many are pretty slim.

## Mammals

In the early days we had otters at Fullers Mill and many water voles, which Bess and I called ferryboats because they were always crossing and recrossing the river. We seldom saw the otters but found tracks and occasionally heard their calls, mostly at night. Then gradually the otters disappeared and so did the water voles, after North American mink had been let out of cages in the New Forest in 1998, by members of the Animal Rights Liberation Movement. The mink quickly established themselves in the riverine environment across the country, killing and devouring moorhens and any living creature they came across, including water voles. Mink are experts in swimming and climbing and in every activity that enables them to get into holes as small as that of the water vole, so they virtually exterminated the species from many rivers. It was only in those large ones near the coast with estuaries that the water voles survived.

Suffolk Wildlife Trust instigated a trapping policy and encouraged landowners and ourselves and our neighbours to collaborate. The original traps were successful to a degree but it was not until the introduction of a floating trap on a raft that the policy really paid dividends. A cover was provided for the raft itself which could be inspected for footprints on the wet mud inside. If these were found, then a mink trap would be put in place with an otter guard on the front to prevent otters getting trapped. After this was set, it had to be inspected on a daily basis and it was found that there was no need for bait since the mink were such inquisitive creatures they would go in anyway and get trapped. This has meant that the recorded incidents of mink in the lakes and rivers have been reduced to negligible numbers. Moorhens are back, as are the water vole. The water voles are still nocturnal, which they become under stress, but as they have several broods a year I am optimistic that numbers can be increased fairly rapidly. Nick Oliver who looks after water voles for SWT comes to Fullers Mill and has seen evidence of water voles on the steep grassy banks which are their chief habitat and where they like to make their tunnels. Otters will eat water voles but because of their size they are unable, unlike the mink, to get into the holes, so they are not a decisive threat. Most evenings I take peelings of apples and pears down to the riverbank and put them out for the voles. Nick says they have a sweet tooth and will sit on the bank and, holding them between their forepaws, eat the peelings. All this is very good news and if only the Environment Agency would set up control measures all over the country mink possibly could be entirely eradicated from the environment.

The future is less positive as regards squirrels. When I first came here there were only Red Squirrels which were a delight, charming little creatures which over the years have been ousted by the larger North American grey version. Simply by being more robust it have taken over the territory, ousting its smaller cousin until now it is totally absent. The Forestry Commission has attempted a reintroduction process but this has not succeeded. It was too little too late to work and there is now no hope of a red squirrel population here anymore.

## Crayfish

As well as mink arriving in the countryside, North American Signal Crayfish were introduced to fisheries in the late 70s because they are larger than our native species, a much more robust animal and just as good to eat. Unfortunately the North American Crayfish (Pacifastacus leniusculus) carried a disease to which they were immune but which seriously infected our native species: the white-clawed crayfish is now very rare on the river if not lost from it altogether.

For a number of years two brothers came up from Newhaven in Sussex to fish for crayfish. They stayed half the week in a caravan locally and stored their catch in keep nets in the river. When the going was good they were catching a thousand crayfish every other day in the summer, from traps with just a mackerel split in half as bait. They used to come every year until in 2011 they discovered that their catch had dwindled; they then visited every other year and now come not at all. They sold their catch at Newhaven fish market where they got a rather small recompense for their work. It was the distributors that sold the crayfish to restaurants, hotels and other retail outlets that made the money. As ever the poor old producer gets less than everyone else in the chain. We welcomed the brothers here because of the devastating effect on our river and fisheries of crayfish eating all the invertebrates, fish eggs and fly lava, and destroying the life of the river. There is now no hope of getting rid of them, only of reducing their numbers. There is no hope at all of our native crayfish returning.

## Thinking about Insects

Thinking back, we used to be troubled by insects in the summer time particularly when we went to bed and turned the light on – there would be masses of insects swarming around. We had a light frame made, covered in muslin which prevented insects coming in so that we could have the window wide open. This we used for many years with great success, but these days the frames aren't needed: there simply are no insects. No matter what the weather, I can have the window wide open, the light on, untroubled by anything. It seems we have killed them all.

When I travelled to Cornwall a year or so ago we were troubled by insects again because there is virtually no cereal agriculture there. There are still a few dairy farms, however, with genuine cows, cattle and cowpats creating storms of insects for swallows, house martins and swifts. Driving home we had to stop and clear the windscreen from smashed up insects which you never have to do in this part of the world anymore. It wasn't until we reached somewhere near Bristol, I suppose, that the insects stopped coming.

For that matter, I don't understand where the milk comes from today either, as there are no dairy farms anywhere near us in East Anglia and they seem to be disappearing from Cornwall too. The farm on which we were staying used to have a traditional dairy herd but the farmer could no longer afford to run it and got more money out of tourism than milk. He converted the milk sheds into holiday flats and it is somewhat ironic to know that where the cows used to graze he has now rented the fields to a Lincolnshire bulb grower who in turn sells his produce to the Dutch who sell them back to the UK as Dutch bulbs!

What a crazy world we have.

## Walking with Cats

In 1998 we got two kittens from the Cats Protection League at Bradfield and called them Monty and Jeannie. They were named after Bess and I had got to know Derek Tangye, the Cornish author of many books on the countryside and in particular about cats. Derek's first cat was called Monty and Jeannie was his wife. Gradually we introduced Monty and

Jeannie to the garden and eventually they would follow us everywhere, even right round the lake, although Bess often had to pick up little Jeannie who had not got the staying power of her brother. Of course we had dogs as well and I have met many dog owners who seem to dislike cats. That is a great shame. They are missing out on one of the joys of keeping small animals because cats are as different as human beings are; they all have their own personalities and one learns how to appreciate them.

After many years of enjoyment, however, Jeannie died and Monty in his turn. He was, I think, fourteen years old. When

this happened the vet asked whether I would like a new cat. He said a stray cat had been brought into the surgery which they were looking after. They were keen to find a home for her. I agreed and she turned out to be a charming little animal, not much more than a kitten although she had already had a family which had not survived. I took her in and named her Jeannie after her predecessor: she is a little charmer with a white front and tummy, marmalade on top with a quaint little face and a deep purr. A very loving little cat.

I have introduced Jeannie to the garden as Bess and I did our other cats. She has proved to have a very good memory or maybe she finds the way by scent because she has only to have been somewhere once and already on the second trip she knows the way. She had a fright on one occasion when I led her down to the lake to feed the wild fowl and to my surprise the pair of swans with their three cygnets were sitting on the bank in the sunshine. As soon as they saw a cat the cob extended its wings fully and hissed which made Jeannie fly for home. For a while she seemed convinced that over the bridges was where fierce swans were permanently sited and she refused to go anywhere near. Now she is well established here, however, she has got over her fright. She comes over the bridges easily and with no problems, but instead of following me, now she is in charge. Once she knows the general direction she leads the way, although with frequent diversions: she gets involved with scents and noises in the bushes and regularly 'kills' the grass and fights it to the death. Then she is off again, climbing trees or rummaging in the garden. She forgets where I am and lets out a plaintive cry. 'Where are you?' she shouts, and I call her back and eventually she comes running. She seems to be aware that my sight is failing and will sometimes come and gently rub against my legs; then I discover she has come back. It makes a walk have hidden excitement for me and I enjoy her presence very much.

On that recent visit to Cornwall I have mentioned I revisited Lamorna and stayed at a farm close by which was within easy reach of the lane going down to the little house on the cliff top where Derek Tangye used to live with Jeannie his wife for whom our cats were named. Jane Bird lives there now. She was one of the Tangyes' early helpers cutting and bunching daffodils from the fields and now rents the cottage from Lord

Falmouth. Among quite a variety of unusual plants, Jane grows camellias to produce evergreens to send up to Covent Garden for flower arrangers and propagates Camellia sinensis to produce replacement plants for the Cornish Tea Company that grows tea on the Fal Estuary. She has a very old cat still at the cottage at Dorminack and a large spaniel that jumps onto her lap, nearly knocking her over as she is quite small. It is hilarious to see and all brings back happy memories of Bess and I visiting Derek and his cat. Walking around the garden here, my brain is full of memories of those happy days.

## Postscript

I have always been interested in the natural world. As a boy I had books, my collections and the expeditions into the countryside with my mother, and as a teenager working in the Brewery in 1940 I used to search out places to look for wild flowers.

At that time I was sent to Lacons Brewery in Great Yarmouth to get further experience of brewing and in my spare time I used to cycle to Brayden Marshes, only a few miles away. The marshes were bordered by Brayden Water, a large expanse of tidal water, so the level would depend exactly on the tide and at low tide it was just hundreds of acres of mud with hoards of different waders from dunlin to curlew and I would go out for an hour of more to study the birds. Here I discovered the owner of a houseboat moored on the water, Robin Harrison, who used to write an article every week in the *Eastern Daily Press* about birdlife. At weekends I would have meals on the boat and study with him. He became my tutor on the water.

I continued to be fascinated by natural history. During the war I added an African dimension to my knowledge. Promotion of the Lackford Lakes Reserve and more recently work with

Suffolk Wildlife's Conservation Committee gave further rein to my enthusiasm. Local initiatives over the years encouraging farmers and village communities to understand, respect and develop the wildlife around them have been as enlightening for me as for the schemes' participants.

However, it is working here, in and with Fullers Mill Garden, that has been the most engrossing and fulfilling expression of my abiding interest. Here I have had my most enjoyable and closest encounters with the natural world. I am very grateful for that.

# Chapter Twelve

# Winding Down

### 'You have col-leek'

Bess was a great walker and one year, perhaps 1968, we decided to do a classic walk in central Norway, the Bessvatnet and Besseggen. It means Bess Water and Bess Edge.

We stayed at the Besseggen Hotel and one fine September morning, sunny and dry, we set off and reached as far as the wooden bridge over the stream which was the outlet of Bessvatnet. We said a few words to some people working there and started on our way round the lake. This was the easy bit: it is a long lake and we were at the far end of it. Soon the northern shore line became broken by big boulders projecting out of the water and we were glad we had special rubber studded boots to be able to leap from one boulder to another and not slip off. With no path, our progress was by fits and starts, jumping from rock to rock not very quickly but safely. Eventually after an hour or two we reached the far end and were able simply to walk along the shore towards the start of the climb on Besseggen. As we began to climb so did the narrowness of the path increase with a sheer drop on the right hand side to another lake way below and on our nearside the slope down to Bessvatnet. The way got narrower and narrower and after about an hour it got so tight that Bess was on her knees, trying as best she could to continue upwards. I managed to stay upright but as we climbed still higher, still the ridge got narrower. It really was rather scary. You looked down to see on either side a sheer face, a boulder strewn drop to the lakes below. How we got to the top I am not quite sure, but we did. By then Bess was terrified, having no head for heights at the best of times, so we paused a bit for her to recover and then set off down on the far side of the ridge to our starting point that morning. Gradually it became easier going and we were able to scramble down until we reached the overflow of Bessvatnet and the bridge by which we had crossed the stream. To our dismay, there was no bridge.

The workmen we had met must have taken it away without saying anything, even though they knew full well that going where we were going led back nowhere except to their bridge. We were in a dilemma. Bess was all for jumping across the stream but I managed to restrain her and so the only other course was to walk down on the 'wrong' side. Again the way was strewn with enormous boulders and rocks but we decided to go down the stream as far as we could. We had to make several detours where the boulders were too big but somehow we managed eventually to get down to a track at the bottom of the mountain. It was now beginning to get dark. We set off along the track, hoping to meet up with the one we used that morning. Thank goodness we did, and were then able to walk back to the hotel.

Well, that evening before we had a meal I felt sick with a great pain in my tummy so Bess went for supper whilst I stayed in bed. I didn't want anything to eat at all. Next morning I was a little better, though I had no breakfast, and by mid morning I felt sufficiently well to start the drive back home. We managed this by stages, finding different places to stay. Although I found it difficult we managed to get as far as Lillehammer and spent a few days there until I got a bit more stable. Then we drove back to Bergen. When we got there I asked my mother-in-law if I could see their doctor.

'Doctor?' she said. 'What do you need a doctor for? You only have a stomach ache, haven't you?'

'I don't know,' I said, 'but I still want to see a doctor.'

'We haven't had a doctor here since Uncle Otto died. You will have to go to the hospital.'

I went there and saw a nice tall Norwegian man who examined me. He started talking to Bess and after a bit I asked him if he could speak in English to me and tell me what the problem was and he said

'You have col-leek.'

'What is that?' I asked.

'It is zee vind,' he replied.

He prescribed charcoal tablets and I thanked him and walked out, not realising (neither did Bess) that we should have paid him on the spot. In Norway you pay first and ask questions afterwards and only if you are unable to pay do you get financial help.

Anyway we took the ferry and completed our journey home, driving from Newcastle, and after a day or two I went to see my own doctor. He said that from all the symptoms I had described, I had had appendicitis and was extremely fortunate not to have died.

'If you will go clambering about mountains you must have your appendix removed. Give it a few weeks to settle down and then we will take you in.'

After the operation and when all this was finished, Bess told her parents what had happened. They had nothing to say, but I hope Uncle Otto at least would have approved of my seeking medical help.

## The Year I was 'kippered'

That appendicitis in the 1960s was my only significant illness in a history of generally good health until, in my seventies, age began to catch up with me.

1999 was the year I was 'kippered' but, to begin at the beginning, several years before my doctor asked me whether I was feeling breathless. I said this happened occasionally and he said we had better get it checked out with a cardiologist. This went on periodically over the years and then one year he said there was a change which ought be attended to. The cardiologist got in touch with a surgeon who worked at Papworth and made an appointment and he said I needed a new heart valve.

'When?' I asked.

'Now.'

'What do you mean now? I am going to Crete in six or seven weeks' time.'

'Perfect,' he said. 'This will get you uphill better than the valve you have now.' I went into the hospital in Cambridge. The last thing I remember is being wheeled into an operating theatre full of people waiting for me and that was where I was split open and cleaned out – kippered. I woke up the next morning in bed with a zip fastener up my chest. It was a very smart way of organising things: in the end you pull all the threads out and the whole thing becomes tight. There was another man in the room opposite mine. I didn't know him but we had lots of mutual acquaintances because he was at Pauls Malt, the maltsters in Bury St Edmunds. We had a lot of time together and I told him stories that made him laugh fit to bust. That was the trouble: it hurt like hell every time you laughed so you needed a pillow by your side which you pressed your chest into whilst laughing. We laughed and laughed and laughed and got each other over the first few very painful days.

Before we were let out they pulled the strings at the end of the zipper which gave quite a jolt and left a nice row of even stitch marks all down my front which are still there to this day. I had no problems walking in Crete but I still have to take a controlled dose of Warfarin to keep the valve clean which is a nuisance. Today you can have an animal tissue valve which for some reason does not have this added requirement.

The Surgeon who did the operation was a charming and very tall Eygptian who came and saw me afterwards. I sent him a couple of bottles of very good claret and like all surgeons he never replied. I don't know why this is but they are all the same in my experience. Maybe it is to do with their insurance.

## Taking Steps

Entering the new millennium, my heart operation slowed me down somewhat, my sight worsened, I needed hearing aids and began to be affected by arthritis. Bess died in 2007. It was time to take stock and make decisions about Fullers Mill Garden.

Bess and I were not blessed with children and so we often talked together about what would happen to the house and garden after we had gone. We decided to investigate turning the garden into a charitable trust. I can't remember exactly what the first move was but I got details from the Charity Commission about how to apply for charitable status. I invited people I knew to join me as the first Trustees. These included John Marshall, who had looked after my tax affairs, as Honorary Treasurer, Colin Hilder, who I hoped would be our first Chairman, Ivan Dickings for his vast botanical knowledge and Colette Barerre for her experience running Alan Bloom's garden at Bressingham. One by one they agreed to become part of the team to run the garden and I then set about applying for charitable status. I got Sir Kenneth Carlisle of Wyken Hall to write a letter in support.

My main theme saw the garden in the context of the closeness of the King's Forest, the Anglo Saxon Village and Country Park and Lackford Lakes Wildlife Reserve. The case I presented was that there was merit in the garden itself, particularly with its collections of Euphorbias and of Lilies, and as part of an area which was becoming of increasing importance as a centre for a wide variety of differing activities, of interest generally to the visiting public. I was told that I could expect a reply from the Charity Commission within several months and that they would then ask me a series of questions in order to evaluate the application. However, to my surprise within two weeks we were granted permission to become a charitable trust. I must have laid it on pretty thick.

One hurdle we had to get over in now establishing the trust was that the firm advising us proved insufficiently aware of all the regulations. Fortunately, I read an article in the weekend *Financial Times* which made it plain that in addition to straight forward Gift Aid you could also give land to a charity which would similarly qualify for tax relief, according to its value. We had discovered this in the nick of time and had a valuation done by Bedfords which enabled us to donate the land in two tranches in two financial years to secure the most benefit.

The Trust was established in October 2004 and for eight years did a pretty good job. Staff were hired, visitor facilities developed and the garden taken in hand anew with the help of a salaried Head Gardener and assistant gardeners and a growing group of enthusiastic volunteers. Some trustees left and others arrived but very little altered as regards the shape of the Trust. However, I had always felt uneasy that we had got no 'Godfather' or larger organisation to help us and, remembering the fate of Maurice Mason's garden among others, I was still anxious about Fullers Mill Garden in the long term future.

Then, in the summer of 2011, I was touring Yorkshire as part of a visit to the Dales and surrounding area when I happened on a small garden near Harrogate called York Gate. It was a sheer delight and very different from our garden since it was clearly designed in the style associated with the Arts and Crafts movement. Then I discovered it had been given by the owners to a charity called the Gardeners' Royal Benevolent Society, now known as Perennial.

I was very impressed by the whole set up, including the people working there, and I asked the lady at reception how I could discover more. She advised me to write to Richard Capewell, the Chief Executive. This I did on coming home and enquired whether there might be some merit in discussing forms of joint membership, to which Richard replied very warmly.

Since then a merger has taken place. I have established a good working relationship with our new owners and I am relieved that Fullers Mill Garden will continue in good hands into the future.

Bernard Tickner
February 2017

# Appendix

# Birdlife and Habitat Change

*This is a listing of birds not introduced in detail in the main text.*

**Avocet**   This is an occasional visitor in the shallows of the old silt beds but I suppose there is not enough food of the right type for them to be there in numbers and this probably applies to all waders.

**Blackbird**   We have a small resident population of these in the garden augmented when the Scandinavian birds come in during the autumn; the bird song in the spring is very welcome and joyful.

**Buzzard**   An occasional visitor but on an increasing scale for those that can see and recognise this distinctive bird.

**Coot**   see **Gadwall**

**Cormorant**   As the lakes grew in number and size a summer roost of cormorants was established in the trees at the east end of the Reserve. It can easily be recognised by the white streaking on the trees. I expect that if numbers continue to increase they will start nesting here but this has not yet happened.

**Cuckoo**   With all the small birds nesting in the reeds on the Reserve we have ideal cuckoo habitat, although I don't know which species is their chief host. There certainly have been a number of cuckoos calling in the early summer months including one that used to say 'cuckoo cuck, cuckoo cuck' which came back for a second year. Occasionally you hear the female calling with its very distinct but un-cuckoo-like notes and very often a male repeatedly cuckooing in an excited manner, as well it might.

186

# A Scratch in the Soil

**Dipper**     This is a rarity and I have only once seen it here because it is out of its normal range. I remember watching it swimming and walking under water, turning over stones in search of insects, disappearing and then reappearing to do its 'dipping', before repeating the process over and again.

**Egret, Little**     In the last few years there hase been an increasing number of Little Egrets here and sometimes on a winter morning I flush one from the pond when we have lowered the level, exposing a good habitat for an Egret. On the coast in Suffolk there are now breeding colonies of these birds and the expectation is that this could happen here, although I am not convinced we have enough shallow water to provide feeding for them.

**Flycatcher, Spotted**     We used to have these year after year. We put up a perch near their feeding place so that we could see them from the dining room windows flying up in the air and returning to the perch, but in recent years they have been amongst the absentees. I think this is the case nationally. They are becoming unusual and maybe rare.

**Gadwall**     are our East Anglian rare nesting ducks and if you can see them close up the males are extremely beautiful although quietly so in a symphony of greys, which suits me being colour blind. I love them. They have quaint ways and I like their treatment of **Coots** - which they use as gardeners. The coots dive and bring up masses of water plants for the young birds and the gadwall just hang around and eat it all. Whether they have each a pet coot would be a nice study for a PhD student writing a thesis on Coot Behaviour.

**Goose, Bean**     We get small numbers of these in most winters and generally they graze like any other grey goose at the east end of the Reserve in the Flempton Meadows – and beyond if there is a crop on the other side of the road, but in spring they are quickly off to the North to breed.

**Goose, Canada**     Over the years the numbers of these have declined sharply here. There is a flock that oscillates between Redgrave, Cavenham pits and Culford Lake and the Lackford Lakes and we used to get many in the garden with their families of goslings making a tremendous mess.

**Goose, Greylag**     With a diminishing Canada population, Greylags have been increasing through the years. Probably of feral origin, they are a welcome addition to the Reserve. At least they are an indigenous species.

**Grebe, Little**    This is a regular breeding species and most welcome for its charming ways, always popping up after longer than expected dives.

**Grebe, Great Crested**    This is another regular breeder and it fascinates with its springtime mating display of neck twisting and show of wing feathers. It is beautiful to watch. They have a habit of carrying their small young on the back of the parent. Once I inadvertently got near to a bird carrying its young and the whole lot dived in alarm and surfaced and dived again. How those little creatures hung on, I don't know. They must have very fast reactions.

**Heron**    There has been a heronry in King's Forest ever since I can remember. Bess and I first discovered it in the days when what is now the Country Park was a rubbish tip. Walking in the forest, we came across a group of trees littered with plastic bags hanging down from the top to the bottom. The herons waited until the tip closed at 5pm and then walked over the exposed face picking up out of date Sainsbury's Chicken Breasts or other waste food. This they carried back to the heronry and fed to their young as easy pickings before just chucking the plastic bags over the sides of the nests. With the closure of the rubbish tip, the herons had to return to working for their living. This coincided with the increase in the number of lakes the habitat provided for them. The heronry itself moved and is now in the pine trees near Wideham Cottages. Today we see the herons coming across the house over to the other side of the river and on to the far side of the Reserve where in the low meadows in the spring there are abundant frogs and toads. Often you hear the heron giving voice as it flies to and fro, especially when the feeding requirements of the young are most pressing.

**Jackdaws**    We have a small colony of Jackdaws nesting in the crevasses and holes in the old Willow trees where they also roost but they never seem to feed here and I think they go to feed with the Rooks from the Fornham Rookery; they go out for the day and return here every night with their chattering and, to me, joyful sounds. I know they are not to be trusted in taking birds' eggs and young but I like them for their pairing for life and for their noisy good humour.

**Kingfisher**   With two hard winters running, Kingfishers have had a bad time here. With the onset of bad weather they seem to clear off to the estuaries where they can fish easily. Fortunately they return in the spring and we generally have at least one breeding pair on the Reserve.

**Nuthatch**   are a great feature in the spring with their calls all day long up in the trees and although I am not able to see them anymore I do enjoy their constant calling.

**Oriole, Golden**   With the colony of Golden Orioles at Lakenheath being the worst kept secret for years I suppose it is almost inevitable that occasionally we get one on passage in the garden and its long fluting calls are unmistakable even if I can't see it. But we never have had them breed here, nor do we expect that to happen as we do not have the habitat for them.

**Owl, Tawny**   Tawny Owls are a feature and I used to be able to call them in with a pretty fair imitation and have had one brush my face but now I am content to hear them calling on a cold night in the moon light. I believe they are a competitor for the Barn Owl and sometimes will attempt to dominate them or even exclude them from the territory.

**Oystercatcher**   These are residents and now breeding on the Reserve regularly. We once had a tame one which must have escaped from someone's collection and would attack visitors' trousers and kick up a tremendous row outside the hides until shooed away to stop it upsetting all the other birds. This was abnormal behaviour, though, confined to this one individual. Oystercatchers are very noisy but cheerful birds. There is no mistaking them.

**Pochard**   are resident and sometimes breed on the Reserve. They do have an attractive way of overwintering as all the females go off to Spain for the winter, leaving the males to tough it out here. This seems to be unlike any other duck. Occasionally we get a Red Crested Pochard which could possibly just be a wild one although I tend to think of them as escapees.

**Pheasant**   These are garden thugs, especially in the early spring when they can smell the bulbs coming out of the ground and with their strong bills dig down to eat crocuses and anemones; we trap them in former coypu traps with a little corn. Occasionally we inadvertently catch moorhens, ironically since it was through them that I originally got the traps when I sought the advice of the Ministry of Agriculture. I went there because at that time in the early sixties we had a plague of moorhens which were killing ducklings by the score. I asked the Ministry man whether he had got any ideas of how to control them and he said

'You've got a lot of coypu at your place, haven't you?'

'No, I haven't,' I replied.

'I'll ask you that question again.'

'Well, yes. We have, since you mention it.'

'Right,' he said. 'You will need a couple of coypu traps on loan to catch coypu.'

I thanked him warmly. I still have the traps today and they catch pheasant.

**Rook**    We do not have a rookery here. In fifty years I have only heard rooks twice and that is in the last two years when, in midwinter, they have gathered to hold a Rooks' Parliament in our trees. You hear them making a tremendous noise, the occasional jackdaw among them, and then it will all fall silent whilst they muster in the tops of the trees before suddenly erupting into a great flying mass above the branches. Then they resettle quietly and the whole process starts again, and again. This apparently is a Rooks' Parliament and what decisions they take I don't know but has been suggested they are planning to build a new Rookery on the site. The nearest rookery which is near the roundabout at Fornham St Martin is very large, extending up the hill for several hundred yards. The trees there have recently been thinned so that it is just possible that the rooks are looking for a new satellite site. I wonder if our jackdaws who roost here have introduced them to this part of the forest. We will wait and see what happens.

**Starling**    To add to what I have written in Chapter 11 about the winter murmuration, starlings are great mimics and I have been caught out by one bird which used to imitate the squeak of the garden gate. I would go out to see who had come into the garden but it was just the starling. They will also imitate birds where they have been feeding and we had one starling which imitated curlews calling. In recent years we seldom get them on the bird table which is quite a blessing because they are greedy feeders.

**Teal**    We have large numbers of teal come in for the winter. This is the smallest British duck, most beautifully marked and one for which I have a great affection. They always come to the same spot in the Reserve where they are able to upend to feed and their presence is always heralded by their cheerful chirrup.

**Thrush, Song**    We have not seen a song thrush here for many years and I deplore this. I think the main cause was the fact that straw burning on the fields was banned and instead the farmers chopped up the straw and ploughed it in. The effect of this was to increase the mollusc population dramatically and to combat all the snails farmers put on tons of Metaldehyde and this, of course, killed song thrushes. It also affected blackbirds which eat slugs killed by Metaldehyde but it did not have such a dramatic effect as that experienced by the thrush population.

**Tits**    We have a full range of tits on our bird feeders, mainly Great Tits and Blue Tits but Coal Tits, occasional Marsh Tits and sometimes Long-tailed Tits come to feed. The latter are a great joy. We even had one that had lost its long tail and looked like a little mouse flying in. Apparently you either get Marsh Tits or Willow Tits but not both in any given area and Willow Tits appear to be absent around here. In the winter occasionally you hear the distinctive 'zing, zing, zing' of the Bearded Tit calling, which is very easy to recognise, and you get good views of them in the thin reeds surrounding the lake. They never breed here as we do not have sufficient reed beds for them.

**Wagtail, Grey**    The Grey Wagtail with its beautiful yellow stomach has nested here for many years in the junipers hanging over the lock wall and sometimes twice in the same season and is often seen on the top of the house on the tiles picking off insects or close by the water taking them as they hatch. I am not sure they are resident but they return each year to breed in the same spot, often fighting their own images reflected in the window of the house.

**Water Rail**    These are resident and breeding birds mostly seen or heard in the wintertime when they let fly with the piercing shriek described as the noise of a stuck pig. Not that that phrase helps me identify them. I imagine it comes from the days of the Raj, when they ran down wild pigs using lances to stick into the poor creatures. Whatever you use to describe it, however, it is a very eerie sound which scares the living daylights out of you in the dusk.

**Woodpeckers**   Both the Green and the Greater spotted are still regular attenders in the garden as we have so many places where they can nest. However, only the Greater spotted comes to the bird table with the Green specialising on lawns, probing with its big bill to find grubs and I suppose worms and ants. The Lesser spotted Woodpecker has not been seen here for a great number of years and often where it does occur inhabits the high canopy and the thickest of woods. It is not an easy bird to see because of its small size, not much bigger than a sparrow, and no one quite knows why it has become increasingly uncommon.